Coaching

Module 7

ASTD Press is an internationally renowned source of insightful and practical information on workplace learning and performance topics, including training basics, evaluation and return-on-investment (ROI), instructional systems development (ISD), e-learning, leadership, and career development.

Ordering information: This ASTD Learning System and other books published by ASTD Press can be purchased by visiting our Website at store.astd.org or by calling 800.628.2783 or 703.683.8100.

Ordering information: This ASTD Learning System and other books published by ASTD Press can be purchased by visiting our Website at store.astd.org or by calling 800.628.2783 or 703.683.8100.

Library of Congress Control Number: 2006920962

ISBN-10: 1-56286-445-9

ISBN-13: 978-1-56286-445-3

ASTD Press Staff
Director: Cat Russo
Manager: Mark Morrow
Associate Editor: Tora Estep
Associate Editor: Jennifer Mitchell
Circulation Manager: Marnee Beck
Editorial Assistant: Kelly Norris
Bookstore and Inventory: Nancy Silva
Marketing Manager: Greg Akroyd
Production Coordinator: Rachel Beuter
Cover Design: Alizah Epstein

Printed by Victor Graphics, Baltimore, Maryland, www.victorgraphics.com.

Table of Contents

1
Conduct Standards

Coaching is a powerful organization and performance development tool. Despite skepticism from those unfamiliar with the coaching experience, the claims for what coaching can do—such as increase productivity, improve quality, strengthen organizations, and retain best employees—are numerous.

Coaches support the learning or performance improvement of an individual through interactive questioning and other means of active input and support. A coach identifies performance gaps, wins commitment to learning, constructs applied practice, and drives continual application and reflection to actually lift competence. A coaching relationship is built on discipline and trust. A coach is a change agent who drives behavior and performance change in a supportive, yet demanding, environment.

Coaching is a service-oriented activity. It is all about the clients and their needs, goals, potential, and barriers to success. Great coaches feel satisfied and fulfilled when they help others succeed. These are the six main purposes of coaching:

1. Improve a client's receptiveness—or so-called coachability

2. Help a client navigate a difficult situation

3. Enhance a client's self-awareness

4. Facilitate breakthroughs

5. Uncover potential and build skills

6. Help create and implement action plans

Learning Objectives:

☑ Discuss the role of the workplace learning and performance (WLP) professional as a coach.

☑ Define coaching.

☑ List several criteria to consider when selecting a coach.

☑ Detail the primary coaching issues with regard to privacy, confidentiality, conflicts of interest, and coaching-relationship limitations.

Role of a Workplace Learning Coach

Coaching is an important aspect of workplace learning because it allows employees to become better workers and communicators. When facilitating a team of learners, the coach usually develops a close rapport with the participants. Because coaching may include managers and executives, the success of coaching can have a tremendous effect on the person being coached and on the organization.

Successful achievement of goals made through coaching can improve career-dependent skills, provide clearer communication, and enable people to make thoughtful decisions.

Not all performance issues can be solved through coaching—just as training can only solve performance gaps due to a lack of knowledge or skill. Coaching is an appropriate intervention if the employee, for example, does not understand the appropriate expectations or priorities or how to correctly complete a task to performance standards. Coaching will not resolve performance issues due to performance obstacles, such as a lack of resources, unrealistic expectations, or too many responsibilities, unless the manager adjusts these external factors.

Definitions of Coaching

Coaching is different from counseling and mentoring. ***Counseling*** is a form of consulting and often is part of a measurement outcome or employee evaluation. Counseling also suggests therapeutic outcomes. Coaching does not do this. Coaching may occur before counseling, instead of counseling, or in addition to counseling. People with a particular expertise conduct ***mentoring.*** This expertise enables them to advise newer or more inexperienced employees.

According to the International Coach Federation (ICF), "Coaching is a professional partnership between a qualified coach and an individual or team that supports the achievement of extraordinary results, based on goals set by the individual or team. Through the process of coaching, individuals focus on the skills and actions needed to successfully produce their personally relevant results."

Coaching is a conversation focused on helping other people (the clients) move forward relative to their goals, hopes, and curiosities. Goals are unmet accomplishments; hopes and curiosities are the rough material of future goals. For coaching to be helpful, it needs to tie to something the clients want to accomplish.

Many people confuse coaching with advice or other business conversations. When people give advice, it may not be welcome. Coaches focus on the clients and the goals the clients want to discuss.

The Coach's Clients

Clients can include managers, peers, employees, or others. A client is someone who has a goal and has sought out help for attaining that goal. Not everyone wants or needs a coach. A highly motivated client generally has a combination of these characteristics:

- eager to succeed
- open to support
- interested in trying different things
- learning oriented.

Mentoring, Performance Management, and Counseling Versus Coaching

Mentoring is a process that helps people with their career development. Mentors provide useful guidance to help people obtain the kind of professional achievement they seek. Mentoring differs from coaching in that it is a longer-term process, and mentors have no responsibility to the participants for personal and professional development. Mentors provide motivation, connections, and advice, but they do not enable participants to directly and substantially improve their performance.

Performance management occurs when managers improve the performance of employees by getting them to take ownership for their performance choices and ultimately the outcomes of their performance. By taking ownership, employees learn to make better choices and, thus, deliver better performance.

Counseling helps people evaluate their behaviors and discover and learn more productive behavior patterns. Employee performance can fall short of expectations for a number of reasons that have nothing to do with the employee and more to do with the organization's systems and procedures. A negative consequence, a missing resource, a lack of training, or a time constraint may prevent optimal performance. Counseling starts by identifying the problem but may require spending more time in the work setting to find out what is really happening.

Coaching is about driving performance development. A coach not only confronts the performance issue and gets the employee to own the behavior choice, but the coach also works directly with the employee, showing how to apply a new skill and enact a behavior to achieve organization goals and objectives. People cannot just change a behavior. They must practice the new behavior with someone who knows how it is done and receive feedback.

The Coach's Purpose and Role

Coaching is usually a part of a larger strategy designed to make major improvements in individual, unit, system, and organization performance. The demand for cultural change or transformation is often associated with these major performance initiatives. Coaching is a tool that is effective and efficient for creating performance improvement and cultural change.

Unlike traditional classroom training, one-on-one coaching allows the coach and the client to focus on issues that the client is facing. It is just-in-time, personal attention.

Hargrove (1995) states, "The primary methodology of masterful coaches is transformational learning." Hargrove's transformational learning has strong parallels with the single- and multiple-loop learning theory used in organization change, which Senge (1990) popularized.

- In *single-loop learning,* people learn and use new skills for necessary but incremental change. For example, learning how to create a project planning document is an example of single-loop learning.

- In *double-loop learning,* the focus is on the fundamental change of thinking patterns and behaviors. People often refer to this act as reframing or changing the context. An example of double-loop learning is learning and practicing effective planning habits.

- In *triple-loop learning,* people make fundamental shifts about how they view themselves and willingly alter their beliefs and values about themselves and about the world (a transformational act). Becoming an inspirational leader who creates and reinforces a culture of planning and execution is an example of triple-loop learning.

A skilled coach supports the employees and the organization by moving easily among the three levels of change. The coach bridges these disparities and helps the employee and the organization align their change initiatives. Table 1-1 outlines key role distinctions between the coach and the client.

Table 1-1. Distinctions Between Coach and Client Roles

Coach's Role	Client's Role
Encourage the client. Reinforce interest in the goals.	Share goals, desired outcomes, and hopes.
Help the client define and clarify goals.	Openly discuss frustrations, problems, setbacks, questions, and successes.
Keep discussions on track and moving.	Share relevant information.
Ask stimulating questions.	Discuss assumptions, opinions, and points of view relative to the goal.
Summarize and clarify discussion topics.	Participate in creating and implementing action plans.
Help the client develop an action plan.	Take ownership of asking for coaching and follow up.

Coach's Role	Client's Role
Offer resources or tools to improve the client's self-awareness or skills.	Review progress to goals.
Facilitate the client's coachability.	Be open to exploring new ideas and approaches.
Make agreements about the next steps and follow up.	Share setbacks and barriers.
Demonstrate a sincere interest in helping the client achieve goals.	Be highly coachable, that is, willing to change and open to suggestion.

Criteria for Selecting a Coach

According to the ICF, the most important consideration when selecting a coach is finding someone the client can relate to. The ICF recommends posing a series of questions to potential coaches, including questions about the coach's education and experience and about the coach's philosophy and process.

Selecting the right type of coach is a by-product of clearly identifying the needs and matching those needs with the right disciplines. Table 1-2 shows how coaching, consulting, training, and counseling distinguish themselves from one another along a range of dimensions. The potential coach and human resource department (HRD) professional are wise to ensure that the needs of the client match the discipline.

Table 1-2. Role Distinctions Among Disciplines

Dimension	Coaching	Consulting	Training	Counseling
The human being	Who the person is	What the person does	How the person does it	Why the person does it
Time	Long-term	Short-term or project	Event or series	Long-term
Focus	Multifocused	Multifocused or single	One or more skills focused	Intra-psychic focus
Future	"Be" in the future or present	Define future and "do"	Learn how to "do" future	Interpret present from past
Human behavior	Mind, body, and spirit	Cognition or thinking	Cognition or thinking	Emotions or feelings
Answers	Answers are inside	Answers (process or product) are provided	Answers are provided	Answers are inside

Discipline Selection

Important differences exist among the four disciplines used to improve human performance: consulting, training, counseling, and coaching. Just as it is vital to know when to hire a consultant (someone who is a subject matter expert—the *what*), a trainer (someone who focuses on skill and knowledge transfer—the *how*), and a counselor (someone who supports resolution of emotional, intrapersonal, and interpersonal issues—the *why*), it is equally vital to know the *when* and *why* for using a coach. Coaching is different from these other disciplines because the other conversations come from the learning leaders' points of view and serve their goals, *not* the clients'. Coaching is the exact opposite. Coaches talk little, listen a lot, and facilitate their clients' thinking processes.

With these distinctions in mind, the needs of the client must first be matched to the right discipline. Yet for the best results for the client, more than one discipline may be required.

The coaching act itself often is an excellent tool for uncovering problems or needs. Coaching helps individuals figure out what they want, what they are committed to, and how much change they are willing to make in themselves and in their organizations. Many successful executives who are not facing any particular crisis or skill deficit turn to coaches for introspection and reflection. The ability to step back, pause, and ponder issues is a valuable resource. This knowledge helps clients use other disciplines more appropriately.

External or Internal Coaches

Individuals who decide to use a coach may have an opportunity to select between an internal and an external coach. An external coach is removed from the parent organization and can offer objective advice. Coaching is often political, especially when the decision maker is at the top of the organizational hierarchy. Coaching naturally requires the development of interpersonal skills, which means that coaches teach people to work better with other people. For this reason, third-party coaches with the right expertise often are the best option.

People often perceive external professionals as having greater expertise and credibility than their internal counterparts because the external professional was hired to produce specific results and thus has a narrow focus for his or her activities. It is a good idea to pass responsibility to the coach to maintain mutual accountability in delivering on the objectives and to stay on track and on budget. The client organization should work with the coach or coaching company to develop a specific plan that details the scope of the work and the objectives, with a budget and timeline. To make a cultural change, the client organization must first target the specifics; otherwise, the outcomes are difficult to verify.

Although an internal coach's knowledge of the organizational culture and formal and informal systems can be an advantage, internal professionals may have dual accountability (for example, to the person being coached and to a supervisor) that can hinder objective and truly client-centered coaching.

For highly confidential and sensitive engagements, an external coach provides a degree of security that may not be easily felt with an internal coach. External coaching offers the learner a safe haven for discussing, exploring, and making decisions about important work-related issues.

Coaching Specialties

External coaches have a variety of specialties. Coaches and clients should carefully consider the kind of specialty coach, if any, that works best for a particular situation. Some common specialty areas are

- small businesses
- entrepreneurs
- executives
- professionals in private practice
- life balance and lifestyle
- creative and fine arts professionals
- women and minorities
- sales professionals
- not-for-profit executives and leaders
- consultants and trainers.

Issues to Overcome When Coaching

One of the coach's goals should be to help improve employee coachability. Sometimes, the coach's behavior turns off the client and gets in the way of the coaching relationship. To ensure that clients are set up for success, coaches must maintain privacy and confidentiality in all conversations during the coaching process. Coaches also must minimize or mitigate any conflicts of interest or elements limiting the coaching relationship.

Privacy

The ability of a coach to interact with his or her clients in private, without interruption, is essential. At the very least, a coach needs to have an area or office appropriate for this activity.

Objectivity and Confidentiality

For any coaching program to succeed, the coach must offer objectivity and confidentiality. Objectivity eliminates politics and often is cited as the reason to hire from the outside. Because external coaches are outsiders, they are unbiased and can focus wholly on the clients' successes. There are no hidden or personal agendas. Confidentiality ensures that all information that is discussed in a coaching session stays there. This has to be the case to ensure that the client fully trusts the coaching relationship. Without trust, no development takes place, and the process will waste time and money.

Conflicts of Interest

According to the ICF's ethical guidelines (for more details, see Chapter 2), coaches must avoid conflicts of interest with their clients. If a conflict—or the potential for a conflict—arises, a coach must openly disclose it and discuss it with his or her client.

Limitations

Coaching can only solve certain problems. It is not a panacea and is not the right solution for every performance challenge or opportunity. Clear expectations, regular performance feedback, and other forms of development are also critical to ensure peak performance. In addition, if the client does not want to receive coaching, it will not help him or her improve. It also may not be the right solution when an entire group of professionals requires the same development, such as when a group requires management development.

Pitfalls of Coaching

Agreeing with the client when another response would be more helpful: Encouraging clients and providing acknowledgment is important. However, coaches should beware of agreeing with clients simply because they get defensive or bothered when people do not share their points of view. This is a tricky situation because coaches want clients to be happy and coachable, but need to provide them with appropriate feedback to grow and develop receptivity.

Being judgmental or rigid: Coaches should avoid being too opinionated. They should feel free to share observations and offer thoughts and concerns but resist stating things in black-and-white terms. Coaches need to be flexible and see setbacks as temporary slowdowns in progress. Coaches should not tell clients that they are wrong or lazy or that their goals are not worthwhile.

Going too fast or too slow for the client: Each client has a different pace. Sometimes coaches have a process that does not allow for flexibility. Typically, coaches should take things slower than the clients. Although exercises, assessments, or planning documents may be available, coaches need to be willing to modify the plan for coaching to suit clients' needs.

Tips for Success

These are some important tips for successful coaching:

- Coaches beginning a coaching effort need to coordinate their activities. They also should choose visible initiatives that can demonstrate successes to get buy-in from top management.

- Managers should provide coaches and clients orientation programs and training that address the concerns, expectations, and benefits to participants and the organizations.

- Individual, group, and organization differences can influence coaching engagements. These influences may determine how the client approaches the process and where the client resides in the organization. (Is the client an individual performer or a member of senior management?)

- Coaches may suggest follow-on activities to help improve performance and increase knowledge between coaching sessions, including research tools, texts, and networking opportunities.

- Competency modeling (essentially a process for identifying a list of knowledge and skills required for a job) and tools for performance improvement may already be in place or may need to be developed from scratch.

- Various methods for collecting and gathering data can be leveraged, including previous coach comments and employee performance reports. The challenge for the coach will be to determine what to do with any information provided.

- Top management support of the coaching program is a critical success factor. Managers should endorse and be willing to fund the program as well as give coaches and clients time away from the job to meet and form relationships.

- Coaches should document the progress of the coaching efforts using evaluation instruments, meeting notes, reports, and logs, and use this documentation to recommend maintaining, expanding, or eliminating programs.

✓ **Chapter 1 Knowledge Check**

1. Which of the following best defines coaching and its primary goal?

   a. The process of addressing individual skill or knowledge gaps

   b. The process of helping people with career development

   c. The process of helping people evaluate their current behaviors and discover and learn more productive behavior patterns

   d. The process of addressing the issues of a particular employee to help achieve organizational goals and objectives

2. A top executive needs help with some processes and strategic decisions that he has not previously encountered. Due to his level in the organization, he prefers to keep his need for coaching in this area confidential. Which of the following is his best solution to keep the coaching sessions confidential from internal resources?

   a. Hire an internal coach from the functional group with knowledge of the processes who has a reputation of being able to keep secrets

   b. Hire an external coach whose results are tied to a specific program

   c. Hire an internal coach from HRD

   d. Hire an external coach but have someone from HRD interview and select the coach

3. Coaching is only conducted one-on-one.

   a. True

   b. False

4. According to the ICF, when selecting a coach questions regarding the coach's education, experience, coaching philosophy, and process should be used to select someone the client can relate to.

   a. True

   b. False

5. Coaching issues may include privacy, confidentiality, and conflicts of interest.

   a. True

   b. False

6. Coaching can solve all performance issues.

   a. True

   b. False

7. The purpose of coaching is to facilitate the client's thinking process.

   a. True

   b. False

References

Brookfield, D. (1986). *Understanding and Facilitating Adult Learning.* San Francisco: Jossey-Bass.

Caudron, S. (October 21, 1996). "Hire a Coach?" *Industry Week,* pp. 87-91.

Darraugh, B. (1990). "Coaching and Feedback." *Infoline* No. 259006.

Finnerty, M.F. (1996). "Coaching for Growth and Development." In R.L. Craig, ed., *The ASTD Training & Development Handbook.* 4th edition. New York: McGraw-Hill.

Fournies, F.F. (1987). *Coaching for Improved Work Performance.* New York: Liberty Hall Press.

Gibson, R.S. (1998). "Selecting a Coach." *Infoline* No. 259812.

Haneberg, L. (2005). *Coaching Basics.* Alexandria, VA: ASTD Press.

Hargrove, R. (1995). *Masterful Coaching: Extraordinary Results by Impacting People and the Way They Think and Work Together.* San Diego: Pfeiffer.

Herzberg, F. (1966). *Work and the Nature of Man.* Cleveland: The World Publishing Company.

Knowles, M. (1984). *The Adult Learner: A Neglected Species.* Houston: Gulf Publishing Company.

Long, J. (2003). "Harness the Power of Coaching." *Infoline* No. 250310.

Lyerly, B., and C. Maxey. (2000). *Training From the Heart.* Alexandria, VA: ASTD Press.

Mink, O.G., K.Q. Owen, and B.P. Mink. (1996). *Developing High-Performance People: The Art of Coaching.* Reading, MA: Addison-Wesley.

Morris, B. (February 2000). "Executive Coaches: So You're a Player: Do You Need a Coach?" *Fortune,* p. 144.

Peters, T., and N. Austin. (1984). *A Passion for Excellence.* New York: Random House.

Senge, P.M. (1990). *The Fifth Discipline. The Art and Practice of the Learning Organization.* New York: Currency Doubleday.

2
Ethical Guidelines

 Coaches understand and adhere to the professional standards and ethical guidelines that govern the coaching relationship. Coaches understand that coaching is distinct from other workplace learning relationships and is a powerful tool for enhancing workplace learning and performance.

The ICF developed a set of ethical standards that all of its members must adhere to. The guidelines are divided into four parts:

- Part 1: the philosophy of coaching
- Part 2: the definition of coaching
- Part 3: the standards of ethical conduct
- Part 4: the pledge of ethics.

The standards of ethical conduct, which are available on the ICF website, include areas of professional conduct at large—including working in a manner that reflects positively on the profession; professional conduct with clients—including guidelines around personal involvement with clients; confidentiality and privacy—including the mandate to respect the confidentiality of clients' information; and conflicts of interest—including the requirements to avoid conflicts and to openly discuss conflicts if they arise.

According to the ICF, "The purpose of these ethical guidelines is to promote professional and ethical coaching practices, and to raise the awareness of people outside the profession about the integrity, commitment, and ethical conduct of ICF members and credentialed coaches." The ICF also has established an ethical conduct review process should problems be found.

Learning Objective:

☑ Discuss how ethical guidelines govern the coaching relationship.

Key Knowledge: Ethical Guidelines

If business ethics are to have a significant influence, ethical business practices require acting in compliance with the rules, customs, and expectations of the business community, which include the business policies of the organizations involved. In addition, to ensure their training and development practices are ethical, WLP professionals must be conscious of the effects of their products, services, or trainer's actions on an organization's employees.

Some organizations have developed guidelines and codes of conduct. These are examples of ethical codes that apply to the practice of coaching:

- The Academy of Professional Consultants and Advisors (APCA) Code of Professional Ethics

- The American Society for Training & Development (ASTD) National Code of Ethics

- The ICF Code of Ethics.

Other standards that relate to ethical behavior are trade practices and self-governing behaviors:

Trade practices: General standards, practices, and guidelines for the WLP industry govern professional activities in terms of behaviors between the buyers and sellers of training and education services. These behaviors are subdivided into three basic activities: contracting, developing, and maintaining. In addition, buyers and sellers should develop practices or guidelines to fit the unique needs of their professional relationships.

Self-governing behaviors: WLP practitioners need to focus on the basic values that will help lead individuals to more consistently ethical behaviors. According to the American Bar Association and the American Arbitration Association, those basic values include

- *honesty:* a personal, objective, and constant commitment to being a witness to truth

- *fairness:* impartiality in all business relationships

- *lawfulness:* observance of both the letter and spirit of the laws governing commerce, individual rights in the workplace, and the expectations of customers

- *compassion:* response to the human needs of others in a personal and moral manner

- *respect:* recognition that all human beings require an understanding of their thinking, the activities in their personal lives, and individual beliefs

- *loyalty:* a sense of personal trust between individuals, among groups of employees, between employer and worker, or between a business and its clients

- *dependability:* consistent personal behavior that meets or exceeds the expectations of all concerned parties.

For more information, see Module 6, *Managing the Learning Function*, Chapter 15, "Legal, Regulatory, and Ethical Requirements."

3
Coaching Competencies

Using and combining the processes of coaching and strategic and tactical action planning addresses individual behaviors, motivation, and related personal improvement. Business coaching focuses on identifying and clarifying goals and emphasizes action, accountability, and follow-through.

Coaching is unique in the manner in which the client interacts with the professional: The client is the driver in this professional relationship because he or she makes the final decision and initiates the appropriate action. He or she is also responsible for abiding by a system of accountability. The coach fulfills the role of a facilitator to fully empower the client. Each client exists within various systems, both personal and professional. These influence how a coaching effort is conducted, as do other factors, such as the organizational culture and structure, available resources, and an organization's business objectives.

Coaching comprises protocols, principles, standards, guidelines, and procedures that contribute to the highest, most resource-effective performance of the discipline and is based on a broad range of experience, knowledge, and practical application.

However, an overreliance on process and protocol can get in the way of the coaching experience and results. If coaches seem more interested in following a specific method or are reluctant to skip steps, clients might lose interest or patience. Problems also can occur when coaches are unavailable for ad hoc coaching. It is important for coaches not to over-schedule their time, thus reducing the opportunities they have to coach. Good chemistry is also a plus; poor chemistry often leads to clients losing interest.

Coaches who focus on what their clients want to achieve can provide coaching that makes a difference. Great coaches are bold and courageous in one moment and reflective and playful in the next. They adapt their dialogs to be most helpful in moving the client forward.

Learning Objectives:

- ☑ Discuss the need for skilled coaches.
- ☑ List the core competencies that effective coaches possess.
- ☑ Explain how establishing strategically aligned objectives and measuring results facilitate learning in a coaching relationship.
- ☑ List and define the basic steps in the coaching process.
- ☑ Explain cognitive dissonance disparity.
- ☑ State the value of mentoring.
- ☑ List the techniques used to create effective communication in a coaching relationship.
- ☑ Describe training and certification programs geared toward coaches.

Setting the Foundation

According to Finnerty (1996), "The changes that have brought about a need for expert coaching skills are connected to the shift from the paradigms of the industrial era to the paradigms of the information age. In the industrial era, businesses hired people for their hands. Today, organizations hire people for their minds. Organizations must have the capacity to quickly respond to the demands created by global competition and rapid changes in technology. Coaching is the management skill that enables organizations to engage the minds of employees."

Finnerty also points out, "Technology creates a demand for coaches. Coaches are needed in an environment where the rapid pace of technological change creates an environment in which employees are constantly learning. Managers can help employees successfully master new tools, programs, or work processes by providing performance observation and feedback. However, many jobs today require greater competence because of the more complex technology involved. Employees need training and coaching to develop the skills to meet these high demands."

Finnerty further notes that managers today are confronted with a workforce that is more responsive to being coached than being controlled. Although employees may lack technological competence, they are better educated as a group. Employees now are expected to participate in problem solving and decision making and use their heads to provide service and improve quality. Employees are less security oriented than those who lived through the depression and world wars. Frankel and Otzao (1992) propose that "today's workers feel that in exchange for coming to work, they should be stimulated, challenged, and recognized for their efforts."

Developing Coaching Competencies

A coach needs myriad skills for a productive coaching relationship. Table 3-1 outlines the critical skills that coaches need and activities that they carry out. The largest category of essential skills is communication, because this is the primary way coaches influence clients to reach the desired goals.

Facilitating Learning

When first instituting coaching as a development strategy, coaches set the parameters for how to integrate and substantiate it and, most important, determine what the client expects to gain from it.

Aligning the coaching initiative with business goals is essential for cultural change; the coach works from the top down and, to get the attention of senior management, demonstrates a direct influence on business measures.

Table 3-1. Most Important Skills Needed to Be a Coach

Skill	Activity
Communication	• Listen • Be direct • Provide feedback • Be empathetic • Ask the right questions • Be quiet • Relate experiences • Provide encouragement • Generate alternatives • Connect information • Engender trust
Client motivation	• Improve motivation for change or action • Facilitate change or transition • Believe in the client's ability • Improve coachability
Self-management	• Be curious • Be nonjudgmental • Have humility • Put aside personal agenda • Be self-aware • Be fully present
Technical skill	• Develop theories of motivation • Implement coaching practices and tools • Increase knowledge of the business • Develop strategies and plans • Create contracts

These are some questions to consider:

- What kinds of outcomes is the client or organization looking for?
- What will the coaching experience look or be like for the client or organization?
- What are the expectations of the coach?

At this point, the coach can determine what to achieve. Coaching can help

- attain a sustained competitive advantage through better performance in specific target areas or competencies
- diminish the expense of firing, hiring, and training new people
- turn around underperforming or derailed executives
- increase knowledge transfer of high performers and exceptional managers
- accelerate leadership capability
- develop a more effective management or leadership succession program
- develop higher-performing projects or cross-organizational teams.

Measuring Results

For the results of coaching to be measurable, the coaching intervention must support specific objectives—this is especially critical when measuring results against business performance. To create measurable objectives, the coach determines the expected outcomes of coaching based on the coaching program's goals and objectives.

Evaluation expert Donald Kirkpatrick's second and third levels of evaluation measure a learner's mastery of content and ability to transfer learning on the job. His fourth level of evaluation measures the results of a training intervention on business measures. Typically, objective level 4 evaluation measures include increased output, cost savings, time savings, and quality improvement, while subjective measures include increased employee satisfaction, employee confidence, customer satisfaction, customer retention, implementation of new ideas, and decreased employee turnover.

By linking the skills and behaviors (level 2 and 3 measures) that the coaching intervention is designed to address and improve to a level 4 measure, the learner and the coach have a focal point and a clear roadmap for on-the-job application.

Understanding the Coaching Process

According to the ICF, "Coaching typically begins with a personal interview (either face-to-face or by teleconference call) to assess the individual's current opportunities and challenges, define the scope of the relationship, identify priorities for action, and establish specific desired outcomes. Subsequent coaching sessions may be conducted in person or over the telephone, with each session lasting a previously established length of time. Between scheduled coaching sessions, the individual may be asked to complete specific actions that support the achievement of his or her personally prioritized goals. The coach may provide additional resources in the form of relevant articles, checklists, assessments, or models to support the individual's thinking and actions. The duration of the coaching relationship varies depending on the individual's personal needs and preferences."

Finnerty (1996) points out that there are many variations on the steps in the coaching process, but all follow a similar format. The steps include

- establishing and sustaining relationships
- communicating expectations and establishing performance goals
- establishing trust
- encouraging development
- identifying resources for success
- observing and analyzing current performance and behavior
- setting expectations for performance improvement
- obtaining commitment, demonstrating desired behavior, and establishing boundaries
- providing feedback on practice and performance
- agreeing on actions and a coaching schedule
- following up to maintain goals.

Establishing and Sustaining Relationships

Coaching requires a safe and comfortable environment that encourages open, two-way communication. Factors that inhibit or enhance the creation of a good environment include the coach's own body language and nonverbal cues. Coaches and clients can send the wrong message by crossing arms (indicating defensiveness), or leaning back to stretch the hands behind the head (a demonstration of superiority).

One of the most important aspects of coaching is the strength of the relationship between the coach and client. This can be a tremendous challenge to WLP professionals who need to coach clients with whom they have not connected. Figure 3-1 shows the various elements of a great dialog. Great dialog begins with **relevance** (the topic is important and makes a difference in clients' lives). Questions must move the topic forward and must be provocative and evocative and lead to **inquiry**. Clients need to feel the **freedom** to share their ideas and thoughts. A sense of **connectedness** should also exist between coaches and clients. In addition, coaches must listen well and provide feedback to ensure **reception** to the ideas presented. Clients also need to feel **empowered** that they have an impact on the topic being discussed. Finally, great dialog is about **play** and a conversation that is fun and full of energy.

Establishing Rapport

Coaching is difficult if this strong relationship does not exist. In establishing a connection, the coach can speed up the process by having deep and meaningful conversations. In cases where practitioners are asked to coach people they do not know well, coaches spend time building foundations for the relationships; this time is well worth the initial effort and will allow the coaches to understand clients' needs and goals more fully and quickly.

Figure 3-1. Elements of the Coach-Client Relationship

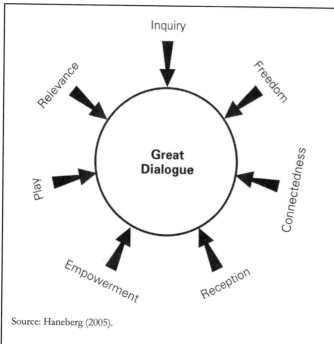

Source: Haneberg (2005).

Spending time establishing rapport and clearly stating the purpose for the coaching session is important. For example, after some friendly conversation, a coach could say something like, "What I would like to discuss with you today is how I can help you be more effective in dealing with irate customers."

If the client does not think that a coaching conversation is relevant, this is a problem. The coach should then have an open conversation about how the client would like to see the meetings change. The coach should try to accommodate the client's hopes while continuing to provide what the client needs to navigate the problem situation.

Asking Questions

Inquiry is at the core of coaching and critical in establishing a productive coaching relationship. People seek coaching because they want to explore and improve their effectiveness and learn more about themselves. Asking questions is a great way to jumpstart inquiry. The two most common types of questions are closed-ended and open-ended.

- *Closed-ended questions* ask for a short or one-word answer: "Do you want to be successful?"

- *Open-ended questions* ask for a longer or individualized answer: "What would it take for you to be successful?"

To create effective inquiry, the coach needs to look deeper than whether the question is closed- or open-ended. Both types can be poor or excellent questions, although open-ended questions involve the client more. The preceding examples are both poor questions. They are not interesting and are too general.

Another way to create inquiry focuses on the quality of the questions asked, in terms of how provocative or evocative they are.

- **Provocative questions** excite and stimulate conversation: "What would happen if…?"

- **Evocative questions** pull in participants and help bring things to mind: "What kind of work makes you feel most engaged and satisfied?"

When the task is more complex, the Socratic method of asking questions is an essential coaching strategy. To help clients develop critical thinking and creativity skills, **Socratic questions** emphasize the use of thought-provoking questions to promote learning (instead of offering opinions and advice). A well-executed Socratic question stretches the mind and challenges deeply held beliefs. Socratic questions are probing and open-ended and can be used in any situation. These are some examples of Socratic questions:

- Why are you saying that?

- What exactly does this mean?

- How does this relate to what we have been talking about?

- What is the nature of…?

- What do we already know about this?

- Can you give me an example?

- Are you saying…or…?

- Can you rephrase that, please?

Using Socratic questions to generate inquiry improves the coach's ability to remain objective by facilitating the client's self-discovery. They help to expand a coach's analysis of the situation and increase the number and the quality of possibilities considered. These questions also increase the energy of the dialog and improve the client's learning.

Communicating Expectations and Establishing Performance Goals

Helping clients clarify their goals is important. Many clients will have only vague notions about their goals. Others will hold onto outdated or unrealistic goals. Some goals will be murky or too broad. Some clients will not know their goals at all. Coaches help craft specific goals that the clients find inspiring, actionable, and meaningful. Goals should be neither too broad nor too specific and should be challenging, but not impossible.

Once the goals have been crafted, coaches help clients create visions for success. Together, the coach and the client should agree about what success will look like and how they will know when it has been achieved.

Once the goals are clarified and defined, coaches help the clients assess the current reality relative to their goals. Coaches ask clients to share the information they have collected, their current results, and their basic assumptions and beliefs about the goals. The end product of this work is a crisp explanation of the clients' goals, how far they are from achieving them, and an idea of their current approaches.

To establish goals, it is important to have a starting point. This can be determined with a self-assessment. The client may try various ways to dodge the issue and accept no responsibility for poor performance. In many cases, the client agrees that a performance problem exists but places blame on someone or something else. Coaches' careful documentation will be of invaluable support, particularly in situations in which clients repeatedly make excuses.

Establishing Trust

The effectiveness of coaching can be crippled if coaches and clients do not feel comfortable about being open and candid with each other. When coaches contract with clients, both parties should agree on how to handle confidential or sensitive topics. Once they have an agreement, sticking to that agreement will build mutual trust and openness.

Coaches will need to deliver feedback that might be difficult for clients to hear. Building positive and trusting relationships and regularly sharing positive feedback will help clients accept the tough messages more constructively.

Encouraging Development

Once clients complete their action plans by establishing performance goals, they will want to get started, if they have not already. Although action is listed as only one step in the coaching process, clients likely will take action during all steps of coaching. Action is a satisfying way to move goals forward. Thus, it is important to ensure that actions are focused and worthwhile.

Identifying Necessary Resources for Success

This may happen earlier in the coaching process, but it often is not cemented until performance goal setting is complete. Once the performance goals are clear, coaching becomes relevant and more tangible. Clients may feel a bit tenuous until their goals are articulated and they understand the focus for the coaching. Coaches should come to an agreement with clients on

- the format of coaching sessions
- the frequency and duration of coaching sessions
- the purpose and scope of the coaching
- the ground rules about confidentiality, candor, coachability, and participation.

Observing and Analyzing Current Performance and Behavior

The goal of coaching is to ensure that clients put forth their best efforts to achieve results. Coaches need to be familiar enough with the clients' jobs to pinpoint potential problems early in the process. This is easier if standards have been preset and agreed on by the supervisor and the employee.

During this step, coaches identify problems, for example, the lack of achievement of a particular agreed-on standard. There are several areas coaches should examine:

- *Role or person match:* The coach should reexamine whether the client is right for the job.

- *Task clarity:* Clients need to know what is expected of them to accomplish tasks.

- *Task priority:* Clients need to know which areas of their jobs are most important. Supervisors telegraph these priorities by the questions they ask and by what they worry about, get excited about, request reports on, use as the basis for promotions, or discuss in meetings.

- *Competence:* Performance problems can be caused by a skill deficiency. Coaches need to separate skill deficiency from will deficiency. Could the client perform this activity if his or her life depended on it?

- *Obstacles:* Real or imagined barriers may interfere with good performance. A printer, for example, cannot maintain high quality in press runs if the press machinery needs maintenance.

- *Reward for failure:* Clients may perceive that they receive more reward for poor or average service—even if it is negative attention—than for good performance.

- *Performance feedback:* Clients need clear, rapid input on how and what they are doing.

- *Valid outcomes:* Part of a coach's job is to find out what motivates clients. Rewards for excellent performance need to be based on what the client values rather than what the supervisor thinks would be a good reward.

To help clients identify possible barriers to success, coaches could ask, "What do you think is preventing you from...?" In this manner, the responsibility is placed on the clients to make them take appropriate ownership. Similarly, coaches should ask what they can do to help. It may be that what the client wants the coach to do is not appropriate or possible. For example, the client may want to go back to doing the task the old way. If that is the case, it is a good starting point for further discussion and maybe even some negotiation. Clients may offer solutions coaches had not considered.

Setting Expectations for Performance Improvement

It is important for coaches to identify the expectations or performance standards and how the client's work does not align with these standards.

Exceptional coaches communicate and measure performance in precise, objective terms. They specify speed (rate), quantity (number or amount), quality or accuracy (absence of errors), thoroughness (completeness), and timeliness (meets deadlines). For example: *The expectation is that you will assemble an average of 100 widgets* (quantity) *per hour* (rate) *with zero defects* (quality).

Effective coaches focus on positive performance that is expected rather than negative consequences. If a coach or manager has not clearly stated the expectations, the client or employee makes the assumption that the standards really do not matter.

One trick of successful coaching is the ability to correct mistakes without causing resentment. In other words, successful coaches provide feedback in a defused manner. Through coaching, unsatisfactory performance is corrected while maintaining the client's sense of dignity and integrity. One error should not call into question everything the client has done or will do. One error does not make the client stupid, clumsy, or bad. An attitude, although it may be difficult to live with, should be tolerated if clients contribute to the best of their abilities to the tasks. In setting expectations, coaches set high standards and, at the same time, are realistic about what they believe clients can achieve.

Solving Problems and Demonstrating Desired Behavior

Sometimes during coaching sessions, clients bring up problems and want the coaches to tell them how to solve the problems. This often is an outgrowth of the self-assessment process. It is more effective, however, when coaches help clients solve their own problems. This approach takes time and requires the mastery of communication skills.

The problem-solving model comprises three parts: diagnosing the problem, generating alternative action or behavior, and identifying consequences for each action.

- *Diagnosing the problem:* The coach asks the client specific questions to help identify real or perceived barriers. The questions should focus on asking what the client thinks might be the problem or obstacle.

- *Generating alternative action or behavior:* The coach asks questions that will help the client think about what could have been done differently. These questions force the client to view the situation from a different perspective.

- *Identifying consequences for each action:* The coach asks questions that focus on possible outcomes of the alternative action. In essence, the coach asks, "What if…" questions of the client.

Sometimes the coach needs to demonstrate the preferred actions through role playing. The coach will assume the role of the client in the scenario, and the client will play the other person involved. For example, if the client needs coaching on how to handle an irate customer, the coach will play the customer service representative and the client will play the irate customer. In that way, the coach demonstrates the appropriate way to handle the customer. Modeling the desired behavior is far more effective than merely telling the client what should have been done or should be done next time.

Agreeing on Actions and a Coaching Schedule

An important part of the developmental coaching process is allowing clients to participate actively in goal setting. People know their own capabilities and limitations. Personal goal setting results in a commitment to goal accomplishment. Coaches and clients should establish performance improvement goals that are specific, realistic, attainable, simple, and time bound as well as strategies for overcoming barriers to achieving those goals. Once again, good questioning techniques help get clients to state what they plan to do to improve performance.

In this step, clients take ownership of the problem and commit to improving performance by stating exactly what they are going to do to improve the situation. Once coaches gain agreement and commitment, they ask clients to summarize the discussion. Coaches should prepare a series of questions in written form for themselves and the clients to follow during the improvement-planning process of the coaching session. This technique provides a way for clients not only to take ownership but also to monitor their progress.

Following Up to Maintain Goals

Successful coaching requires an action plan and follow-up. Coaches state precisely what clients need to do. As a best practice, coaches ask clients to summarize sessions by stating what they are going to work on. Also, good coaches ask what they can do to support the clients in their efforts to improve performance.

Before concluding the coaching session, the coach and client must agree on a time to meet to discuss progress. The next meeting should be scheduled to give ample time for the client to practice the skill or behavior, but not so much time that he or she assumes the matter is forgotten.

Coaching takes time, practice, and patience. To guide clients through this process, coaches need to remember that effective coaches practice the five Rs—respect, reinforcement, recognition, reward, and role modeling—to develop clients into peak performers.

Once a client has learned the skills through initial training, the employer might believe the job is complete. Not so! The next phase is on-the-job coaching, an ongoing process generally performed by the client's supervisor. Peer coaching also is being used more frequently, particularly in team environments and especially within self-directed work teams. Coaching is a continual process designed to enable the client to gain greater competence and overcome barriers to improving competency once he or she has the knowledge or skills to perform job tasks. Coaching encourages clients to do more than they ever imagined they could and is appropriate when clients have the ability and the knowledge to do the job but are not meeting performance expectations.

Providing Feedback

Central to the coaching process is giving feedback. When done correctly, feedback is a valuable tool to help the client improve performance. If done poorly, feedback can demotivate and, in some cases, destroy the client's self-confidence.

There are two types of feedback: evaluative and developmental.

- *Evaluative feedback* focuses on the past and is designed to grade the client's performance, such as in a formal performance-appraisal process.

- *Developmental feedback* focuses on the future and is designed to help the client raise performance or prepare for the next level of effort.

When giving feedback, coaches use I-messages instead of you-messages. I-messages are statements about behavior and resistance to communication. You-messages that blame, accuse, or attack the other person cause clients to respond emotionally and negatively.

Feedback Guidelines

For feedback to be effective, coaches follow a set of guidelines to elicit appropriate and productive responses from their clients:

Ask clients to self-assess performance: For coaching to be effective, clients have to buy into the process. One way to promote the collaborative aspect of coaching is to ask clients to evaluate their own performances. When they identify areas for improvement, they are more likely to make the commitment to improve.

Be descriptive rather than evaluative: Coaches focus on behaviors that can be observed, measured, or discussed objectively and describe them. Good coaches do not put clients on the defensive by generalizing or making assumptions.

Be specific, factual, and actionable rather than general: Coaches describe the behavior in the context of the actual situation. Not only should feedback describe observable behavior, but it should be stated in the context of specific incidents or situations. Useful feedback is direct, honest, and concrete.

Discuss only behavior clients can change: Some clients have shortcomings they cannot change, or there may be circumstances or situations beyond their control. These topics should not be discussed, because clients cannot improve on them.

Consider the coach's and the clients' needs: This approach ensures clients' egos, self-esteem, and rights remain intact. Coaches must strive for win-win situations.

Communicate clearly: Coaches must check for clarity by asking clients to state their understanding of discussions.

Ask questions rather than make statements: Coaching is about aiding clients toward self-discovery by allowing them to evaluate their own actions and behaviors.

Feedback Guidelines, continued

Comment on the actions that clients did well, as well as areas for improvement: This will boost clients' confidence and encourage them to try harder in their performance goals.

Observe personal limits: Coaches should not give too much feedback at once.

The responsibility for keeping the lines of communication open rests with coaches who deliver the messages honestly and focus on behavior description, not evaluation. A behavior is something the client does that can be observed, measured, and discussed objectively. A coach can discuss attitudes based on observed behaviors.

Because I-messages communicate how coaches experience clients' behaviors as well as the consequences of the behaviors, clients are more likely to accept the coaches' comments as positive and constructive. Feedback is more effective when it immediately follows performance. It should be relevant to the task and should provide the client with information on how to improve task performance. Feedback can be either positive or negative, and clients often complain that the only time they receive feedback is when they do something wrong.

Positive feedback also should be specific. It is not enough to tell clients that they are doing well. A much more effective and meaningful comment would be, "Maria, I like the way you handled that difficult customer. You showed a great deal of restraint and professionalism by not raising your voice or losing control."

Identifying Coaching Opportunities

Coaching provides many performance improvement opportunities, but not every employee is a candidate for coaching. Those who are not open to feedback or do not seek coaching are not likely to benefit from it. One way to improve coachability and coaching effectiveness is to focus on possibilities, strengths, and the employee's goals for success. This approach works more effectively than focusing on problems and weaknesses. Basic theories of motivation, such as *Maslow's hierarchy of needs* and *McGregor's theory X and theory Y of management,* should guide coaching practices. Maslow's theory says that motivation in humans is driven by both lower-level needs (food, drink, sleep, and sex) and higher-level needs (belonging, love, and self-actualization). McGregor further refined these concepts to apply specifically to motivation in work situations. As individuals, employees are motivated by senses of belonging, accomplishment, and personal mastery. Coaching that improves intrinsic motivation will be most effective.

People change when current practices cause more pain and dissatisfaction than other approaches would. To facilitate change, coaches stimulate conversation and understanding about the reasons to change and the consequences of sticking with the status quo. To fuel and enrich the learning process, coaches should expose clients to a diversity of thinking and approaches. When clients are open to and interested in input from various people, cultures, and disciplines, they think better, act more effectively, and produce results.

Coaches help clients succeed by keeping the end, their clients' goals for success, in mind. It is critical to clearly define the desired outcomes, short-term milestones, long-term milestones, measures of success, and action plans. Client- and goal-focused coaching helps individuals and organizations grow and succeed.

Using Facilitation Methods and Cognitive Dissonance

At times throughout the coaching process, clients may experience *cognitive dissonance.* It is imperative that coaches help clients through this condition and discover the true feelings of clients.

Cognitions are defined as attitudes, emotions, beliefs, or values. When contradicting cognitions exist, the *cognitive dissonance theory* indicates that this conflict serves as a driving force that compels the human mind to acquire or invent new thoughts or beliefs or to modify existing beliefs. These new or modified thoughts and beliefs minimize the amount of dissonance between cognitions. A key skill of effective coaches includes drawing out these conflicts when working with clients to help lead them down a path to correct the inappropriate actions or behaviors.

Several facilitation methods and techniques help to solicit and clarify the true meaning of what clients say in the context of their desires. One way to solicit this information and get clients to participate is to ask open-ended questions. This use of effective questioning techniques will get clients more involved in the process and, in turn, lead to greater commitment. Open-ended questions help the coach gain valuable insight into clients' thinking. In a training situation, closed-ended questions test clients' understanding of a particular process or procedure. Open-ended coaching questions go deeper. Coaching requires a mode of questioning more oriented toward solving problems. Examples include "What do you think is getting in the way of…?" "What have you tried to do to…?" or "How can I help you improve your…?" Asking clients to "Tell me more about…" is a powerful way to encourage them to expand their comments. Questions starting with "why" should be used with caution because they risk coming across as challenging and may cause clients to become defensive.

After asking open-ended questions, effective coaches employ active listening techniques to encourage clients to open up even more. Many coaches fail in their coaching efforts because they spend more of their time talking in a coaching session, telling clients how to handle the situation differently instead of asking questions and really listening to clients.

People confuse hearing and listening. Studies show that, at best, people listen at only a 25 percent level of effectiveness. Hearing is physical; it happens when people's ears sense sound waves. Listening, however, involves interpreting, evaluating, and reacting.

Listening is the process of taking in information from a speaker without judging, clarifying what the listener thinks he or she heard, and responding to the speaker in ways that invite communication to continue. Listening is one of the most important, most underused, and least understood coaching skills. When someone really listens to a speaker, he or she typically feels respected and appreciated. When a person senses that others are listening to him or her and trying to understand his or her viewpoint, the person begins to open up and drop barriers. The result is a climate of trust, openness, and mutual respect that leads to greater cooperation and better coaching results.

When actively listening, to ensure that coaches correctly understand and interpret what clients say, they should summarize what was said, paraphrasing or reiterating and mirroring what clients said. When disparities occur between clients' thoughts, feelings, and actions and the desired performance or behavior, coaches should help to clarify the disparity and lead clients to the appropriate conclusions.

Techniques that facilitate communication during the coaching process include

- clarifying to confirm understanding of what is being said
- setting goals
- using questioning techniques, such as open-ended and Socratic questions
- brainstorming
- mind mapping
- role playing to explore alternative ideas and solutions and to lead clients to self-discovery.

Enhancing Coaching With Technology

Many technology-based tools can enhance a coaching practice. As businesses become more global and geographically dispersed, in-person coaching may not be practical or possible.

Although meeting in person is optimal, these are some other ways coaches can connect with clients:

- **Phone:** Coaching sessions can be conducted over the phone and are particularly suited to sessions where visuals are not needed.

- **Voice over Internet Protocol (VoIP):** Many companies use VoIP as a regular communication tool. With VoIP, coaches can contact clients anywhere they have an Internet connection. Another advantage of VoIP is that many programs allow file transfer, which allows coaches to send documents back and forth as they talk without having to send a separate email.

- **Online meeting programs:** As travel becomes more expensive and less desirable, many companies use online meeting platforms to have virtual meetings. This is a great coaching option; it also is a good tool for small team-coaching sessions.

- **Email:** Although coaches should not rely on email for all coaching, it is a good tool to keep in touch with clients between meetings. Coaches should send follow-up emails after each coaching session to clarify and reinforce agreements made during the session. Coaches should also forward interesting articles or blog posts to clients.

- *Goal-setting and project-management software:* If clients are familiar with project-management tools, coaches can incorporate them. There are many project-management and goal-setting programs to choose from.

By using various tools and methods for coaching, coaches improve communication effectiveness and serve their clients better. New technology is created for coaches each year; coaching newsletters and periodicals that cover coaching often list these latest developments.

Considering Coaching Certification and Training Programs

As coaches develop their practices, they may consider whether coaching certification programs are right for them. Several national programs and many universities offer coaching certificates. Each program varies in length and depth. Coaches should weigh their needs, available time, and resources before selecting a program.

The ICF offers three levels of its Certified Coach credential: the Associate Certified Coach, the Professional Certified Coach, and the Master Certified Coach. Each level of certification requires a certain number of coaching and training hours. These programs are for professional coaches only.

Many other organizations offer training programs, which range in length and depth, as well as training for coaching certification. Coaches also may find degree programs and individual classes at local universities.

For most internal positions, a coaching certification is not required, but it might help coaches compete for open positions. Certification is more likely to make a difference in large companies or for external coaching practices. It is important to continually build skills as a coach, and organizations will want to see that coaches have taken the initiative to become exposed to a variety of resources and coaching models. As coaches build their coaching practices and create their personal development plans, they should consider a variety of training options.

Understanding Mentoring

It is ironic that in this time of technological achievement, the lifeblood of corporations is the accumulated insight of the people who choose to give their gifts of talent and commitment to any given organization. So, the question is this: How do organizations ensure that the intellectual legacy of employees continues?

A large portion of the answer lies with mentoring initiatives. Mentoring is a powerful, dynamic process—for both employees and organizations. To share wisdom is to share life experience. Mentoring has the potential to elevate corporate dialog from the mundane to the truly transformational. Mentoring is not for everyone, and a mentoring program will not solve all training needs. It is an ongoing process that provides an opportunity for a mentor to share skills, knowledge, and experience with a protégé.

Mentoring can take several forms, from an informal relationship in which a mentor helps a protégé learn a specific task to a long-term relationship in which a mentor provides advice and support to a protégé over a period of several years.

There are some common misconceptions about mentoring and mentoring programs. Mentoring is not

- an opportunity for an experienced employee or manager to tell a protégé what to do

- a one-way relationship in which all benefits accrue to the protégé

- a working relationship without difficulties or challenges

- a working relationship in which the more experienced person always has the skill sets

- a substitute for other types of learning through classrooms, e-learning, and personal networks.

Through mentoring programs, protégés develop vision and expertise and mentors become invigorated, knowing that they are leaving a legacy to their organization, profession, and community.

A key benefit to mentoring programs is that they offer something other career development programs do not—individual attention. Traditionally, organizations have been interested in grooming employees to take over jobs of increasing responsibility. On another level, they might be concerned with retaining the bright, young graduates who could easily take their skills and enthusiasm elsewhere if they are not quickly involved in the excitement and goals and with the people of the organization.

Organizations often look toward a formalized mentoring program as a means of instituting a management continuity system at a variety of levels. Some use the program to groom middle management for senior-level jobs. Mentoring programs are an effective means of increasing the political savvy, exposure, and visibility middle managers need if they are going to succeed in top-level management positions.

Structured Mentoring Versus Traditional Mentoring

Table 3-2 outlines the key differences between structured mentoring and traditional mentoring. These key differences are important considerations for helping organizations decide whether structured mentoring or traditional mentoring programs will meet their needs. To establish which kind of program it needs, an organization should consider the following situations for which structured mentoring programs tend to be more effective and efficient than traditional mentoring programs:

- A person has just joined the company and needs to learn specific skills as well as the social context of the work. (Structured mentoring is particularly important for a new college graduate.)

- A person has changed jobs in the company and needs support during the transition, such as in expanding a personal network in the new position.

- A person is being groomed for a promotion.

- The task is more than the sum of its parts, such as in consulting or management, where both knowledge and soft skills are critical to job success.

Table 3-2. Distinctions Between Structured and Traditional Mentoring

Structured Mentoring	Traditional Mentoring
Time limited, focused on the protégé's acquisition of a particular skill set, usually within a particular context	Long or short term, depending on needs of the protégé and willingness and availability of the mentor
Focused on specific behavioral objectives	Focused on career development and overall career performance from a long-term perspective or over a period of time
Clearly articulated expectations for both mentors and protégés	Used by corporations to assist employees in learning and adhering to certain corporate requirements
Planned activities created for the purpose of providing the protégé with an opportunity to learn specific skills in a specific context	Unplanned activities that come up on the job and are not created specifically for the purpose of learning
A means for structured feedback from the mentor	Lack of structured means for feedback; feedback is provided, but the quality and quantity depends on the mentor
Active engagement of the protégé in reflection and self-assessment	General absence of reflection and journaling; self-assessment may or may not be present, but mentor mostly provides feedback
Inclusion of an evaluation component to document business results	Metrics and an evaluation component may or may not be present

✓ Chapter 3 Knowledge Check

1. Which questioning technique seeks to develop critical thinking and creativity skills?

    a. Open-ended

    b. Closed-ended

    c. Socratic

    d. Didactic

2. Which of the following is most appropriate for gaining experience in a specific job role and having formal, standardized documentation ensuring competence and the ability to complete the function appropriately?

    a. Coaching

    b. Executive coaching

    c. Mentoring

    d. Structured mentoring

3. During the analysis stage of the coaching process, which best describes the coach's focus?

    a. Identifying the problem and lack of achievement of a particular agreed-on standard

    b. Creating the performance metric standards

    c. Documenting observations and establishing performance metric standards

    d. Identifying the negative and positive consequences and current reward systems

4. Which type of feedback focuses on the future and is designed to help the client raise performance or prepare for the next level of effort?

    a. Evaluative

    b. Developmental

    c. Formative

    d. Summative

5. The responsibility for building and keeping the lines of communication open in a coaching relationship rests with the client.

    a. True

    b. False

6. The primary purpose of having an employee self-assess his or her performance is to build

   a. Trust

   b. Confidentiality

   c. Factual observation

   d. Commitment

7. According to the ICF, coaching always begins with a face-to-face personal interview to assess an individual's current opportunities, challenges, and to define the scope of the relationship and priorities.

   a. True

   b. False

8. Factors that inhibit or enhance the creation of a good environment include the coach's own body language and nonverbal cues.

   a. True

   b. False

References

Biech, E., and M. Danahy. (1991). "Diagnostic Tools for Total Quality." *Infoline* No. 259109. (Out of print.)

Dent, J., and P. Anderson. (1998). "Fundamentals of HPI." *Infoline* No. 259811.

Finnerty, M.F. (1996). *"Coaching for Growth and Development."* In R.L. Craig, ed., *The ASTD Training & Development Handbook*. 4th edition. New York: McGraw-Hill.

Fournies, F.F. (1987). *Coaching for Improved Work Performance*. New York: Liberty Hall Press.

Frankel, L.P., and K.L. Otzao. (Autumn 1992). "Employee Coaching: The Way to Gain Commitment, Not Just Compliance." *Employee Relations Today*, pp. 311-320.

Haneberg, L. (2005). *Coaching Basics*. Alexandria, VA: ASTD Press.

Herzberg, F. (1966). *Work and the Nature of Man*. Cleveland: The World Publishing Company.

Kaye, B., and D. Scheef. (2000). "Mentoring." *Infoline* No. 250004.

Kirkpatrick, D.L., ed. (1998). *Another Look at Evaluating Training Programs*. Alexandria, VA: ASTD Press.

Lawson, K. (1997). *Improving On-the-Job Training and Coaching*. Alexandria, VA: ASTD Press.

Thomas. S.J., and P.J. Douglas. (2004). "Structured Mentoring: A Performance Approach." *Infoline* No. 250401.

Willmore, J. (2004). *Performance Basics*. Alexandria, VA: ASTD Press.

Appendix A
Glossary

Career Development is a planned process of interaction between an organization and an individual that allows the employee to grow within an organization.

Coaching is a process in which a more experienced person, or coach, provides a worker or workers with constructive advice and feedback with the goal of improving performance. (See also *Mentoring*, which focuses on career development and advancement.)

Cognitions are attitudes, emotions, beliefs, or values.

Cognitive Dissonance Theory states that when contradicting cognitions exist, this conflict serves as a driving force that compels the human mind to acquire or invent new thoughts or beliefs, or to modify existing beliefs so as to minimize the amount of dissonance between cognitions.

Counseling helps people evaluate their behaviors and discover and learn more productive behavior patterns.

Developmental Feedback focuses on the future and is designed to raise performance or prepare the person for the next level of effort.

Double-Loop Learning focuses on fundamental change of thinking patterns and behaviors. People often refer to this act as reframing or changing the context.

Evaluative Feedback focuses on the past and is designed to grade performance such as in a formal performance-appraisal process.

Facilitation refers to the role of the WLP professional who guides or makes learning easier, both in content and in application of the content to the job.

Feedback is advice or information given from one person to another about how useful or successful an event, process, or action is. In coaching, feedback is given to clients regarding their progress, which helps with retention and behavior.

ICF (International Coach Federation) is a nonprofit, individual membership organization formed by professionals worldwide who practice business and personal coaching.

Intervention is another word for a solution or set of solutions, usually a combination of tools and techniques that clearly and directly relate to closing a performance gap.

Learning is the process of gaining knowledge, understanding, or skill by study, instruction, or experience.

Maslow's Hierarchy of Needs refers to Abraham Maslow and was introduced in 1954 in his book *Motivation and Personality*. Maslow contended that people have complex needs such as physiological (food, drink, sex, and sleep) needs, safety/security, social/belongingness needs, esteem, and self-actualization, with the basic needs having to be satisfied before an individual can focus on growth.

Mentoring is the career development practice of using a more experienced individual tutor or group to share wisdom and expertise with a protégé over a specific period of time. There are three types of mentoring commonly used: one-on-one, group, and virtual.

Model is a representation or example of an idea, object, process, or phenomenon used in describing ideas and processes.

Objective is a target or purpose that, when combined with other objectives, leads to a goal. The following are some examples of particular types of learning-related objectives:

> **Affective** learning objectives specify the acquisition of particular attitudes, values, or feelings.

> **Behavioral** objectives specify the particular new behavior that an individual should be able to perform after training.

> **Learning** objectives are clear, measurable statements of behavior that a learner demonstrates when the training is considered a success.

Observation occurs when participants are directed to view or witness an event and be prepared to share their reflections, reactions, data, or insights. This also is a methodology for data collection.

Single-Loop Learning refers to a type of learning in which people learn and use new skills for necessary but incremental change.

Structured Mentoring is time limited and focused on the protégé's acquisition of a particular skill set and on specific behavioral objectives.

Traditional Mentoring is long- or short-term and focused on career development and overall career performance from a long-term perspective and/or over a period of time.

Training Objective is a statement of what the instructor hopes to accomplish during the training session.

Triple-Loop Learning refers to a type of learning in which people make fundamental shifts about how they view themselves and willingly alter their beliefs and values about themselves and about the world (a transformational act).

Transfer of Learning describes the process of learning delivery, retention, and implementation back on the job.

Workplace Learning and Performance (WLP) refers to the professions of training, performance improvement, learning, development, and workplace education. It often is colloquially referred to as training or training and development.

Appendix B
Answer Key

Chapter 1

1. Which of the following best defines coaching and its primary goal?

d. The process of addressing the issues of a particular employee to help achieve organizational goals and objectives.

2. A top executive needs help with some processes and strategic decisions that he has not encountered previously. Due to his level in the organization, he prefers to keep his need for coaching in this area confidential. Which of the following is his best solution to keep the coaching sessions confidential from internal resources?

b. Hire an external coach whose results are tied to a specific program

3. Coaching is only conducted one-on-one.

b. False

4. According to the ICF, when selecting a coach questions regarding the coach's education, experience, coaching philosophy, and process should be used to select someone the client can relate to.

a. True

5. Coaching issues may include privacy, confidentiality, and conflicts of interest.

a. True

6. Coaching can solve all performance issues.

b. False

7. The purpose of coaching is to facilitate the client's thinking process.

a. True

Chapter 3

1. Which questioning technique seeks to develop critical thinking and creativity skills?

c. Socratic

2. Which of the following is most appropriate for gaining experience in a specific job role and having formal, standardized documentation ensuring competence and the ability to complete the function appropriately?

d. Structured mentoring

3. During the analysis stage of the coaching process, which best describes the coach's focus?

a. Identifying the problem and lack of achievement of a particular agreed-upon standard

4. Which type of feedback focuses on the future and is designed to help the client raise performance or prepare for the next level of effort?

b. Developmental

5. The responsibility for building and keeping the lines of communication open in a coaching relationship rests with the client.

b. False

6. The primary purpose of having an employee self-assess his or her performance is to build

d. Commitment

7. According to the ICF, coaching always begins with a face-to-face personal interview to assess an individual's current opportunities, challenges, and to define the scope of the relationship and priorities.

b. False

8. Factors that inhibit or enhance the creation of a good environment include the coach's own body language and nonverbal cues.

a. True

Appendix C
Index

Appendix D
Case Studies

Coaching Makes an Unexpected Difference

Global Telecommunications Firm

By Madeleine Homan, Linda Miller, and Scott Blanchard

A business unit of a global telecommunications firm engaged Coaching.com to provide a series of coaching sessions for 67 of its employees. The participants in the coaching process included all sales managers from the executive level to district sales managers. This intervention began early in 2001 and concluded for most participants in May 2001. It was the express intention of the coaching intervention to deliver results against the following key business objectives:

- demonstrated increase in leadership capability

- improved alignment to achieve key responsibility areas

- measurable increase in the areas of retention, productivity, and value sales versus commodity sales.

A third-party study performed three months after the coaching revealed that the coaching intervention had produced significant business and economic impact, specifically in improved retention, improved work environment, increased productivity and revenues, and decreased erosion of the customer base.

Organizational Profile

The client organization was a field sales division within a significant business unit of a global telecommunications company. Operating in more than 65 countries, the company offers Internet, voice, and data solutions that make businesses more productive, secure, and cost-effective. As measured by revenues and traffic carried, this organization is the leading global data, Internet, and network services provider. It generated revenues of $22.8 billion in 2001. Based on all forms of traffic, the organization carries more data over its networks than any competitor.

The field sales division, which was the client group, had had four successful years providing one percent of the company's overall revenues but four percent of its profits. The field sales division's era of hockey stick growth was slowing down, and it needed to move from an entrepreneurial environment to a mature process-oriented environment without losing passion and energy. The organization had 600 employees, 38 district sales managers, 11 regional sales managers, eight sales directors, five sales operations managers, and a vice president of sales.

Background

The training professionals who invited Coaching.com to discuss their business needs originally found out about Coaching.com on the Internet and expanded their research through conversations with the director of coaching services. A meeting between the client organization's two training directors and Coaching.com staff revealed a potential fit of service to business need. The vice president and senior leader of the client organization attended the meeting, and there was consensus that the organization did not need more training. (The organization had already invested significantly in Situational Leadership II, a key product of Coaching.com's parent company, The Ken Blanchard Companies.) Instead, the organization was interested in something fresh that would allow individuals to get what they needed to move forward. There was a great deal of synergy between the two companies, particularly since both actively use telephone and Internet technology to ease communication. This commonality immeasurably increased understanding and the impression of "fit." Once the business needs were understood, Coaching.com proposed a combined solution that included consulting services and coaching services.

Project Design and Implementation

Scope of Work and Objectives

The client organization agreed to use Coaching.com to do the following:

- develop key responsibility areas (KRAs) and impact maps for 11 of the client organization's positions. Impact mapping is a process that begins with identifying organizational goals, and then identifies and defines the strategic competencies that are critical to the achievement of those goals by job role

- provide orientation to, practice with, and apply the standard Situational Leadership II (SLII) One-on-One Forms with individual coaching clients

- help individual clients to emerge from their final coaching sessions with a completed professional development plan around their interviewing and recruiting practices, and with completed impact maps based on their KRAs

- increase usage and application of SLII with coaching clients, based on individual coaching

- provide general business coaching services to improve quality management practices and leadership skills and behaviors. A series of 10 coaching sessions (two sessions lasting up to one hour and subsequent sessions lasting up to 45 minutes) was provided to each manager over a four-month period.

Coaching.com agreed to provide consulting services (development of KRAs and impact maps for 11 positions, customized for the client organization) and project management services as needed. Coaching.com also agreed to provide the following individual coaching services:

- conducting individual coaching services with the client organization managers to achieve improved quality and quantity of one-on-one meetings with their direct reports

- assisting the client organization's managers with the completion of their individual impact maps, with the express purpose of aligning individual development plans, KRAs, unit goals, and business goals

- facilitating the completion and documentation of personal development plans, including, but not limited to, more effective use of SLII skills, utilization of effective hiring and selection practices, and improved frequency and quality of one-on-one meetings

- during sessions one and two, provide an orientation to the coaching process and the platform, with the first session to include management history and experience, assessment of SLII training, review of current important issues pending for the individual, and discussions regarding goals for the coaching experience

- during sessions three through 10, complete the self-assessment used on the Coaching.com website. This trademarked Scrubdown process requires the client to decide that something is either true or not true, on the premise that clients will work on and be willing to change things about which they are currently telling the truth. Sessions three through 10 also included a review of the KRAs and impact maps, application of SLII practices, review and practice with the one-on-one process, and completion of the impact maps and individual development plans.

Finally, Coaching.com agreed to generate reports to track the project.

Monthly administrative reports reviewed important aspects of the coaching sessions from the data collected every week. The following trend data had to be reported by one third or more clients to ensure anonymity and confidentiality:

- qualitative written data describing the themes that had emerged during coaching sessions, which had resulted in shifts of perspectives or attitudes

- qualitative written data regarding the client organization's processes and policies that were or were not working

- qualitative written data regarding the discrepancies between the client organization's leaders' actions and words

- quantitative data regarding the number of sessions coaching clients had completed or missed, and if any clients had dropped out

Project summary reports included an overall review based on the data presented in monthly reports.

The Coaching Process

Clients

Prior to their first sessions, the clients participated in an orientation designed to explain the following:

- what coaching is and is not
- why their company was investing in coaching
- what they could expect of their coaches and their coaching experiences
- what was expected of them
- the level of confidentiality they could expect
- logistical aspects involved in scheduling, using the Coaching.com Internet platform, cancellations, and coach/client mismatches.

During this orientation, participants heard about some early wins that their leader had experienced with his own coaching, which had started earlier by design. After the orientation, they used their log-on names and the passwords they had received with their Coaching Guidebook to navigate the Internet to the Coaching.com platform to take their Scrubdowns. They then used the automatic scheduler to set their first sessions with their coaches.

Once the clients were off to a good start with their coaches, they could choose to use a prep form on the Internet platform to focus themselves and prepare their coaches for their upcoming sessions.

Coaches

Coaching.com coaches used the same basic process with each client. Prior to the first session with the client, the coach used the Scrubdown Calculator, a tool that uses information from the client to identify potential issues and focus areas. If there were focus areas that were unfamiliar to the coach, he or she could read up on the subject from the materials on the website.

During their sessions with their clients, coaches did the following:

- established relationships with clients, assessing style and approach
- reviewed basic "housekeeping" details as needed
- debriefed Scrubdown experiences and reviewed responses
- discussed potential areas of focus for work together
- assessed "brushfire" areas that could be causing too much distraction and needed to be handled immediately
- connected to larger strategic focus areas where applicable

- discussed and clarified the confluence or opposition of personal goals with corporate objectives
- reviewed the impact maps and assessed areas for development.

At the end of each session the coach would ask a variation of the following to make sure that value was perceived:

- What will you take away from this session?
- What do you know, see, feel, or realize now that you hadn't before our session?
- What will you do differently moving forward?
- Is there anything you need to say to feel grounded, clear, and purposeful?

Over the course of later sessions the coaches continued to drill down into focus areas, setting clear SMART (specific, meaningful, attainable, relevant, trackable) goals, brainstorming and deciding on action steps, and reviewing activities for effectiveness. Accountability was offered according to client need as appropriate.

Measurement and Evaluation of Coaching Program

The following is an excerpt from the "Impact Evaluation Report on the Coaching.com Intervention." The study and report were designed and completed by Triad.

It was the expressed intention of the coaching intervention to deliver results against key business goals. The purpose of this impact evaluation was to determine whether those results were produced, why and by whom, and if not, why not.

Background and Methodology of Study

The investigators used a "success case" methodology that sought to answer these questions:

- What business impact has this coaching intervention produced?
- What is the economic value of that impact to the client organization?
- When coaching produces a business impact, what contributes to that outcome?
- When participants do not see a business impact from their participation, why not?
- What can the client organization do differently or better to increase the impact of similar interventions that might be offered in the future?

The "success case" methodology uses a two-step approach to gathering impact data.

Step One: An impact map was created for each job role to determine how coaching participants could use the coaching process to produce business impact. A survey based on that map was intentionally structured to help identify participants who claimed the most success in using the coaching process to produce positive business impacts.

The survey was emailed to 59 coaching participants. Fifty participants returned completed surveys, for a return rate of 95 percent. Figure 2 presents the survey, and figure 3 shows the results.

Figure 2. Coaching initiative-impact survey.

Directions: Select your response to each question by clicking on the radio button for your answer. When finished, click on the Submit button. Your responses will be treated confidentially. Thank you!

1. When I began participating in the coaching sessions, I had very clear goals for my participation.

☐ Strongly Disagree ☐ Disagree ☐ Agree ☐ Strongly Agree

2. The coaching sessions helped me better understand what I needed to change/do differently if I was going to help achieve our business goals of increasing employee productivity, protecting current pricing, retaining the best employees, deeper account penetration, etc.

☐ Strongly Disagree ☐ Disagree ☐ Agree ☐ Strongly Agree

3. My coaching sessions gave me the skill and confidence I needed to do things that were important to achieving my own and my company's goals.

☐ Strongly Disagree ☐ Disagree ☐ Agree ☐ Strongly Agree

4. I have learned some things about effective coaching from this process that I am already using with my direct reports.

☐ Strongly Disagree ☐ Disagree ☐ Agree ☐ Strongly Agree

5. My manager was extremely supportive of my participation in this coaching process.

☐ Strongly Disagree ☐ Disagree ☐ Agree ☐ Strongly Agree

6. Overall, the impact that the coaching sessions have had on my own and my company's business goals has been:

☐ Very Low ☐ Low ☐ Somewhat ☐ High ☐ Very High

After completed surveys were returned, the investigators strategically selected individuals for in-depth interviews. For "success cases," the selection criteria included the following respondents:

- those who selected either "high" or "very high" when asked to rate the business impact of the coaching intervention

- those who were equally distributed by region of the country, by job role, and gender.

"Low success cases" were selected using the demographic criteria. On the question of overall positive impact from the course, these individuals rated the business impact of the coaching intervention as "low." The investigators interviewed each of only three of 55 respondents who selected this response.

Figure 3. Results of the coaching initiative-impact survey.

Q.1 When I began participating in the coaching sessions, I had very clear goals for my participation.

Choice	Count	Percentage Answered
1. Strongly Disagree	1	1.8%
2. Disagree	17	30.9%
3. Agree	29	52.7%
4. Strongly Agree	8	14.5%

Q.2 The coaching sessions helped me better understand what I needed to change/do differently if I was going to help achieve our business goals of increasing productivity, protecting current pricing, retaining the best employees, deeper account penetration, etc.

Choice	Count	Percentage Answered
1. Strongly Disagree	2	3.6%
2. Disagree	5	9.1%
3. Agree	29	52.7%
4. Strongly Agree	19	34.5%

Q.3 My coaching sessions gave me the skill and confidence I needed to do things that were important to achieving my own and my company's goals.

Choice	Count	Percentage Answered
1. Strongly Disagree	0	0.0%
2. Disagree	3	5.5%
3. Agree	33	60.0%
4. Strongly Agree	19	34.5%

Q.4 I have learned some things about effective coaching from this process that I am already using with my direct reports.

Choice	Count	Percentage Answered
1. Strongly Disagree	2	3.6%
2. Disagree	2	3.6%
3. Agree	23	41.8%
4. Strongly Agree	28	50.9%

Q.5 My manager was extremely supportive of my participation in this coaching process.

Choice	Count	Percentage Answered
1. Strongly Disagree	2	3.6%
2. Disagree	2	3.6%
3. Agree	22	40.0%
4. Strongly Agree	29	52.7%

Q.6 Overall, the impact of the coaching sessions on my own and my company's business goals has been:

Choice	Count	Percentage Answered
1. Very Low	0	0.0%
2. Low	3	5.5%
3. Somewhat	11	20.0%
4. High	29	52.7%
5. Very High	12	21.8%

Step Two: Using the role-specific impact maps as guides, in-depth interviews were conducted with survey respondents who had reported either high or low impact from the coaching. These interviews took between 20 and 40 minutes. In some cases, investigators received permission to talk with direct reports and managers of those interviewed to corroborate the stories they had shared.

Using all of the data from the surveys and the nine "success case" and three "low success case" interviews, the investigators arrived at the key findings and recommendations that follow. These are supported by multiple data sources, including all survey and in-depth interview data; they are never based on comments or data from a single source or only a few sources.

Key Findings

The Coaching.com intervention produced significant business and economic impact. Both the survey data and the in-depth interviews provided ample evidence that this intervention produced, and will continue to produce, significant impact. Specifically, the investigators found abundant evidence that this intervention contributed directly to these KRAs:

- Top-performing staff had been retained.

- A positive work environment had been created.

- Revenue had been increased by moving formerly average performers to a point at which they were exceeding their plans. A revenue increase may be too much to expect, given the company's year-to-date revenue levels. However, this conclusion is not about the company's revenue but about the way in which the coaching intervention helped managers work more effectively with targeted individuals. The accurate question would be: "How much farther below plan might the company have been if the coaching initiative had not been in place?"

- Reduced erosion in customer-based revenues and customer satisfaction occurred due to the ability to fully staff territories more quickly when vacancies occur.

Figure 4 gives a breakdown of the economic impact of coaching.

Figure 4. Economic impact of coaching.

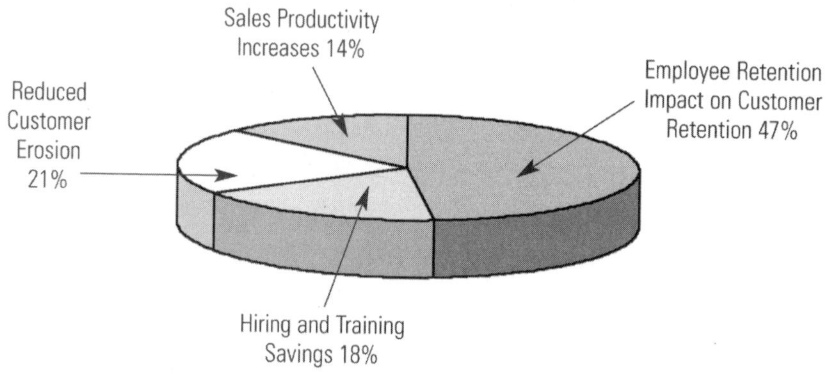

The intervention will have long-lasting impact on the client organization's people and business. Fully 92 percent of all survey respondents indicated that they had learned coaching techniques they are now using with their direct reports; Figure 5 shows the results. Thus, the impact has had a cascading effect in the organization. A coaching approach is a very powerful way to develop a highly accountable, empowered workforce that is quick to respond to opportunities that provide high levels of customer satisfaction. A consulting approach is typically driven from the top and is slow and not very responsive to customers. In this intervention, participants experienced the power of the coaching process and found themselves receiving great benefits. It proved so beneficial that participants are willing to use the process with their reports. The long-term impact will be significant.

Figure 5. Percentage of respondents who benefited from coaching.

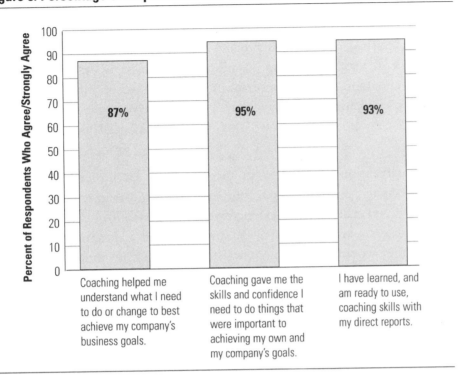

There was confusion on the part of participants about whether they were working with a coach or a consultant. At the beginning of the process, many participants wanted the Coaching.com coach to tell them what to do in response to a specific need. Initially, the refusal of the coaches to do this frustrated some participants, but most discovered that the coaching process was about their discovery of solutions. They appreciated that the coaches stuck with the coaching approach because they felt as if they ended up owning the actions and were excited to see how they played out.

The process did not have a clear exit strategy. Many participants were uncertain about the next steps, if any, that would follow their 10 coaching sessions. Most participants suggested that they would like to have had an account of three to five more coaching sessions that they could schedule as needed over the next six to 12 months. Managers suggested that it would be helpful if they could have an account of 20 to 40 coaching sessions that they could make available to their direct reports on an as-needed basis. These messages meant that participants found great value in this process and wanted to have more sessions available, but to be used as they determined.

Participants wanted more control over the scheduling of their sessions. A significant number of participants thought they needed to have a coaching session each week for 10 weeks. After the third or fourth session, many would have liked to schedule their next sessions based on need or have more time to take the actions they had planned in their most recent sessions.

Sponsorship of this initiative at the executive level of leadership in the organization made the business impact more likely. The level of engagement of senior leaders in this coaching process was highly effective, contributing significantly to its success. Individuals talked about how engaged their leaders had been in this process and how often they had been asked about progress and how it was helping the business. These messages from management made the coaching intervention visible, important, and worth investing in with time and energy. This also led to a significant level of internal discussion among participants about their coaching experiences and the process. This further reinforced the value of the intervention.

The timing of this intervention contributed to the high level of business impact. The coaching intervention taking place during a time of changing organizational structure, reporting relationships, and sales processes increased the business impact. The client organization's staff members asked very hard questions about their commitment to the client organization; whether they would fit into the new structure, roles, and processes; and what level of anger they should direct toward the organization if they felt the changes were unfair or inappropriate. Having a third-party coach available during this time helped many individuals work through the above issues and, in fact, helped them move through the organizational changes with greater commitment to the client organization, to their work, and to their managers and direct reports. Specifically, participants said they were able to discuss some of these tough issues with their managers, some of whom effectively coached direct reports who were considering leaving the client organization. Quite a few participants found their personal commitment to the client organization changed for the better.

Participant openness to the coaching process made a decided difference in the personal and business impact that was achieved. Those who reported the highest levels of personal and business impact were excited by the coaching opportunity. In fact, a number of those interviewed indicated that they had considered engaging a personal coach or mentor before this coaching initiative was announced. They perceived the client organization's commitment to this process as very positive and could not wait to get started.

The three out of 55 respondents who reported little business impact perceived the process as a time for them to meet with a "shrink" because they were not performing well and needed help. These individuals were unable to take full advantage of the coaching process.

Significant business and personal alignment among individuals and within teams occurred as a result of the coaching intervention. Individuals frequently reported that they used their coaches to help them solve less-than-ideal working relationships with their managers or with one or more of their direct reports. Many commented that the use of the impact maps, especially with their direct reports, brought significant alignment on critical business issues. Others indicated that they found themselves talking and working with their managers much more effectively. In these cases, their coaches had helped them develop approaches and strategies to bring about the desired change. In one situation, a manager used his coach's support to help two employees whose competitiveness was causing their team to function poorly. Both are now working effectively together and exceeding their individual plans.

This intervention demonstrates how people and performance can be positively changed using a process and not an event. When a performance improvement intervention is spread over time and built into the doing of the job—as this intervention was—very positive results can be expected. Had this been one intensive 10-hour experience, the impact would have been only a small fraction of what was produced. The coaching process allowed participants to work on new behaviors over time, create shifts in perspective that otherwise might not have occurred in the classroom in two days, and integrate their coaching into their jobs, rather than just learning about coaching. The client organization and Coaching.com used a very powerful process that produced significant business value.

A neutral third-party coach proved valuable at several levels. Participants in this intervention described how they had talked with their coaches about issues that they had difficulty raising with their managers or direct reports, ending up with plans, strategies, and options for raising those difficult issues.

When third-party coaches begin working in organizations, there is often a concern that this process might drive a wedge between persons being coached and their managers. This evaluation proved quite the opposite. Instead of separating the manager and direct report, the process served to bring them together, helping them to become aligned with key business goals and bringing about more effective working relationships.

The third-party coach also provided a safe haven in which to try ideas and approaches, build confidence, create strategies for raising concerns and problems, and bring about clarity and support among staff. Because the coach was not connected to the client organization, the participants were confident that there was no underlying agenda on the coach's part. They saw their time with their coaches as a "free discussion zone." However, it should be noted that coaches did not allow "gripe" or "victim" sessions, but focused on personal accountability and action.

Closing Thoughts

The vision of Coaching.com is to democratize coaching in organizations, using the best that all technologies have to offer. After years of working with individuals, the company suspected that the impact of coaching on individuals would improve the bottom line if coaching was delivered on a large scale in organizations. Now there is proof.

Although it wasn't relevant to coaching objectives, the client organization went through a reduction in force and reorganization in the middle of the coaching initiative. The anecdotal evidence that coaching provided much needed relief for those undergoing inordinate stress is abundant. One evening the sponsor called and used the term "divine intervention" about the serendipitous fact that 14 Coaching.com coaches happened to be serving in his organization at a time of such intense change. The experience for us as coaches and tireless advocates for coaching was profoundly moving.

Questions for Discussion

1. If you had a chance to re-create the coaching initiative outlined—with the objectives—what would you change in the original design?

2. How were the sudden reduction in force and reorganization factors in the success of the coaching?

3. In your estimation, was the assessment of economic impact fair?

4. How might the economic impact have been measured differently?

5. What was it about the coaching that made such an impact?

The Authors

Madeleine Homan, chief coaching officer and founder of Coaching.com, was the head coach on this project. With more than 12 years of coaching experience, Homan was an original advisory board member and senior trainer at Coach University and recently served as the vice president for professional development for the International Coach Federation, of which she is a founding board member and from which she earned the master certified coach designation. Homan's responsibilities at Coaching.com include design of coaching initiatives; coaching content and process development; and oversight of the staffing, training, and development of coaches. She can be reached at Madeleineh@coaching.com.

Linda Miller is vice president of coaching services at Coaching.com and was the senior coach on this project. Since joining the Coaching.com team in 2000, Miller has been responsible for developing coaching infrastructure, deploying coaches, and overseeing all implementation of major client initiatives. Miller has coached and trained corporate leaders and their teams at companies such as Allied Signal, Boeing, Deloitte and Touche, Delta Faucet, Duke Energy, and US West. Miller is a founding recipient of the master certified coach designation from the International Coach Federation and is a member of the National Speakers Association.

Scott Blanchard is CEO and founder of Coaching.com and was the lead consultant for this project. Blanchard serves as a director of the Ken Blanchard Companies. He is an experienced business consultant, trainer, and speaker. Prior to the creation of Coaching.com, he helped manage large training initiatives in the financial services, automotive, software, telecommunications, retail, and service industries. Scott holds a master's degree in organization development from American University.

Source: Adapted from D.J. Mitsch, ed. (2002). *In Action: Coaching for Extraordinary Results.* Alexandria, VA: ASTD Press.

The Return-on-Investment of Executive Coaching

Nortel Networks

By Merrill C. Anderson, Cindy Dauss, and Barry F. Mitsch

Nortel Network's Leadership Edge program is focused on developing future leaders for the company. Coaching was a key component of Leadership Edge from the start, and informal testimonials of clients who had been coached had been very positive. However, once the coaches had completed the first engagement for Leadership Edge, the company asked, "How successful is coaching in delivering real value to the business and how can coaching be better leveraged in the future?" A groundbreaking study applied proven measurement methodology to document the financial and intangible value of coaching. This study provides critical insights into how coaching creates value in an organization and includes ideas on how to maximize the business value of coaching.

Organizational Profile

Nortel Networks is a multinational telecommunications company that operates in more than 150 countries. With more than 40,000 employees worldwide, the company specializes in providing communications technology and infrastructure for Internet, voice, and multimedia services. Nortel controls close to 90 percent of the North American broadband market, with close to 75 percent of all Internet traffic riding its optical network. The company also has leading market positions in wireless technology.

Background and Strategy

Nortel Networks is committed to developing its leadership capability in order to meet the demands of the challenging telecommunications industry. Leadership Edge was created to accelerate the development of next-generation leaders. Participants in the program are selected and sponsored by their business units based on their performance and the leadership potential they have demonstrated. They come from diverse global functions, including sales, marketing, technology, human resources, and finance, and represent a range of professional levels, from individual contributor to mid-level manager.

The development strategy for Leadership Edge involves formal assessments, including 360-degree feedback and personalized development planning in which coaching is a key component. Nortel Networks contracted with the Pyramid Resource Group (PRG) to provide coaching and coaching support services for the Leadership Edge program. PRG specializes in corporate coaching and provides a staff of certified coaches with extensive business backgrounds. Coaching gives participants the opportunity and the freedom to work privately with professional coaches who are skilled at helping individuals increase their overall effectiveness and leadership competency. Because the coaches come from outside the organization, participants are more willing to share their challenges and concerns without fear of potential consequences.

The coaching process began with a live orientation program. Potential coaching clients were also electronically provided with information to introduce coaching and establish expectations. Following orientation, a coach matching process was conducted by PRG, with input from Leadership Edge managers. PRG reviewed available assessment documents for each coaching client, conducted phone interviews with the clients, and then selected the most appropriate match from its team of senior coaches.

The coaching engagements lasted for five months, with two hours of telephone coaching each month. Coaches were available for email and phone check-ins as needed by their clients. During the program, coaches provided reports to PRG's project coordinator on the progress of each engagement and any trends they were observing with their clients. A comprehensive trends report was submitted to Nortel every three months to help the company assess progress. The information in the trends report was consolidated so coach/client confidentiality was protected.

Following completion of each coaching engagement, Nortel conducted a level one evaluation of the process. Qualitative feedback gathered by the Leadership Edge coordinator was used to report back to the Nortel managers who were overseeing the overall Leadership Edge program.

Although participants spoke highly of their experience with coaching, Nortel Networks and PRG determined that a formal assessment of the business impact of coaching would facilitate future decision making when choosing among developmental alternatives. Therefore, they commissioned MetrixGlobal to conduct this study with the intention of understanding the following:

- how coaching added value for Nortel Networks, including the financial impact of coaching

- how Nortel Networks could best leverage coaching in the future.

Figure 1 shows the process that was used to analyze return-on-investment (ROI) for the coaching.

The Coaching Study

Data Collection Procedures

A questionnaire and follow-up interview were used to isolate and capture the effects of coaching on the business. Delivered electronically, the questionnaire examined participants' initial reactions to coaching, what they had learned, and how they had applied what they had learned. It also captured an initial assessment of business impact. The follow-up phone interview probed the potential financial ROI. This approach provided a consistent method of exploring the unique nature of each client's experience with coaching and how this experience translated into business benefits.

Figure 1. The process used to analyze ROI for the coaching.

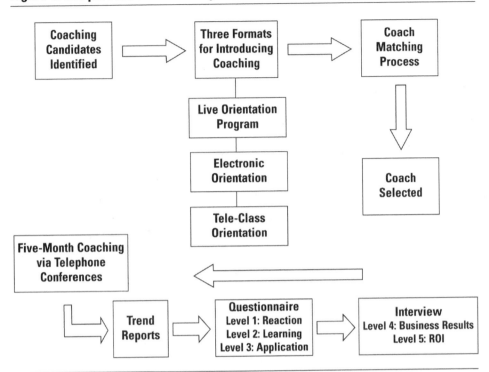

This study focused on six levels of data analysis (Kirkpatrick, 1977; Phillips, 1997):

- *Level one:* initial reaction of the clients to their coaching. The more positive the clients' initial reaction to coaching, the higher the likelihood that they will later experience valuable learning.

- *Level two:* what clients learned from coaching. This demonstrates the extent to which the clients have gained the knowledge and insights they need to make meaningful enhancements to their performance.

- *Level three:* how clients applied what they learned. The more frequently and effectively clients apply what they have learned, the greater the likelihood of their having a positive impact on the business.

- *Level four:* the business impact of coaching. This shows how the changes that the clients have made created value for the business.

- *Level five:* return-on-investment. It is important to know not only the total financial benefits of coaching, but also how this total compares to the total program cost.

- *Intangible benefits:* Not all benefits can be documented in financial terms. However, because such intangible benefits as customer satisfaction are valuable to the business they are noteworthy.

Profile of the Respondents

Forty-three Leadership Edge participants were surveyed for the MetrixGlobal study; 30 responded, for a response rate of 70 percent. Most respondents reported having leadership responsibilities in such roles as people management, project management, and team leadership. Functional responsibilities included sales, finance, marketing, technology, and human resources. More than one-third of the respondents (37 percent) had direct customer contact as part of their job responsibilities, and 43 percent had direct reports. All but four were based in the United States. The average tenure with the company was six years, and 11 (37 percent) of the respondents were female.

Not all Leadership Edge participants received coaching. For the most part, coaching was provided to those people who requested it, but a few coaching respondents reported feeling pressure to participate. The study reinforced the need to provide a more formal introduction to coaching and ensure that participants understand the voluntary nature of the offering.

Measuring Impact

The results of the coaching study are described below, along with detailed discussion of the findings from each of the six evaluation levels.

Level One: Initial Reaction of the Clients to Their Coaching

As figure 2 shows, one-third (33 percent) of the respondents were initially skeptical that coaching would make a difference for them. Many of these respondents reported that they did not initially understand what coaching was or how it was going to help them. These issues, however, were not significant given the high ratings that both clients and coaches gave the initial two or three coaching sessions. According to 90 percent of the clients, these initial sessions provided a strong foundation for the coaching as objectives were set (90 percent reported favorably) and rapport was established (97 percent).

Level Two: What Clients Learned From Coaching

Figure 3 shows that almost all respondents (97 percent) gained critical insights into personal changes that they needed to make in order to be more effective. For 93 percent of them, this included realizing how to improve communication and collaboration skills. Eighty-three percent cited a better understanding of how to work with peers to accomplish business objectives. Gaining greater understanding of their personal impact on others (77 percent) and finding new ways to look at business situations (77 percent) were also cited as valuable outcomes.

Overall, almost three-quarters (73 percent) of the clients learned how to be more effective as leaders.

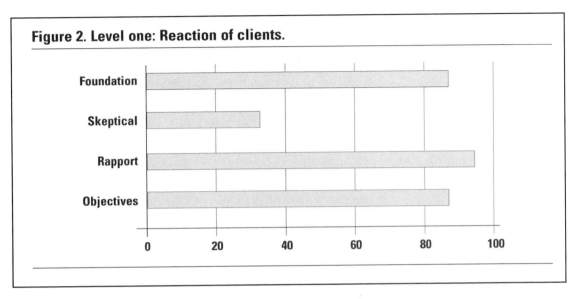

Figure 2. Level one: Reaction of clients.

Coaching sessions were characterized by the clients as rich learning conversations that fostered self-examination. Having the coaches come from outside the company was considered a benefit: Clients appreciated the relative safety of the coaching relationship, in which they could privately explore how to handle business situations. Many clients said that the coaching had enabled them to more rapidly develop as leaders and, in some cases, to develop differently as leaders. As a result of coaching, leadership styles were reported to be more inclusive of others' needs, less defensive, more supportive, and more focused on top priorities. Many clients reported being more careful in approaching situations and problems, more open to new ideas and alternative solutions, and—for those with customer contact— more effective with customer interactions.

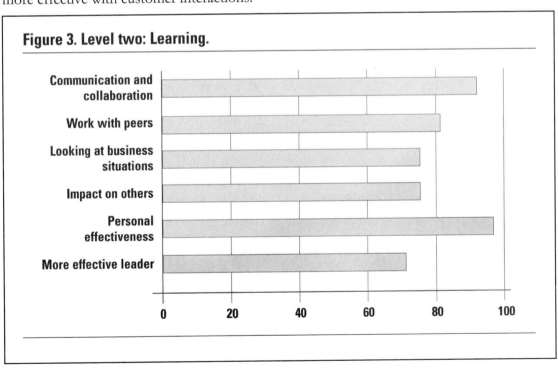

Figure 3. Level two: Learning.

As Figure 4 shows, seven of 10 clients were better able to handle real-life business situations as a result of the coaching they had received. Given the unique nature of each coaching relationship, the particular business situations addressed varied from client to client, but most (70 percent) were able to apply what they had learned during coaching to positively influence a business situation. More than half of the clients (53 percent) were better able to motivate others to accomplish business objectives. At least four out of 10 clients (47 percent) improved the quality or speed of decision making and were more effective working on business projects (43 percent). More than one-quarter of the clients applied their learning from coaching to improve team performance (30 percent) and to better utilize people and money (27 percent), and 13 percent reported increased retention of team members.

Additional applications for coaching included engaging others more effectively, dealing with restructuring, defining objectives and creating action plans to achieve these objectives, and better managing work/life balance.

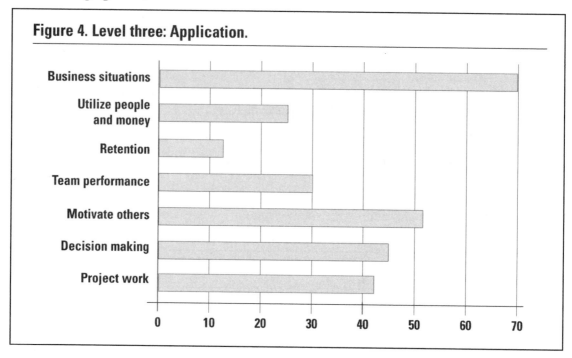

Figure 4. Level three: Application.

Level Four: The Business Impact of Coaching

Three-quarters (77 percent) of the respondents indicated that coaching had significant or very significant impact on at least one of nine business impact areas that were measured as a part of the study. During in-depth discussions conducted by telephone, more than half (60 percent) of the respondents were able to identify specific financial benefits from coaching.

Figure 5 presents the nine business impact areas and shows the percentage of respondents who cited each as significantly affected by coaching. The figure also shows the percentage of respondents who cited financial benefits and the total financial benefits for each business impact area. The comments section provided additional information about the benefits documented by the participants.

Figure 5. Summary of financial impact.

Business Impact Area	Percent Citing Significant Impact	Percent Identifying Financial Benefit	Comments
Work Output	30%	20%	Benefits generated as a result of higher output of self or team through enhanced decision-making, collaboration, and accelerated achievement of objectives.
Work Quality	40	0	It was not possible to quantify these benefits and so, although substantial, these benefits will be considered intangible.
Productivity	60	50	Personal or team efficiency benefits expressed in terms of hours saved per week. Assumptions included $75 per hour, 48 weeks a year.
Cost Control	3	3	Reduction in sales and general and administrative expenses.
Product Development Cycle Time	10	0	Few respondents were involved in managing product development.
Employee Retention	27	13	Four team members said that they would have left Nortel Networks without the coaching. Three other team members said that coaching significantly influenced their staying with Nortel, but these three were not included in the benefits calculation. Two respondents mentioned retaining team members. These benefits also were not included.
Employee Satisfaction	53	0	This benefit was the second-most cited of all benefit categories; however, it was not possible to quantify this benefit in financial terms. This is another significant source of intangible benefits.
Customer Satisfaction	33	0	Most respondents who had customer contact indicated that customer satisfaction likely increased as a result of their changed behavior (due to coaching). This benefit was not directly measured and is considered an intangible benefit.
Sales Volume	10	10	Benefits are margin contributions to Nortel Networks (not total sales increases), based on 25% margins.
Total Financial Benefits			Financial benefits are not total benefits, but rather isolated benefits due to coaching.

Overall, participants cited personal or work group productivity and employee satisfaction as most significantly affected by coaching. More than $250,000 in documented annualized productivity benefits were recorded. Employee satisfaction could not be quantified but represented a significant intangible benefit to the company. As a result of the coaching, the participants were more satisfied and better able to increase the work satisfaction of their team members.

Work output and work quality were also cited by respondents as significantly affected by coaching: Nearly $1 million in increased work output for themselves and their work teams was documented. Because many respondents reported improvements in work quality but were not able to quantify these in terms of financial benefits, work quality improvements were considered an intangible benefit of the coaching.

The customer satisfaction and sales volume increases cited as influenced by coaching translated into increased net revenue; fixed cost reductions were documented by one respondent. Reductions in product cycle time were not identified as a benefit in this particular study, as no respondents were involved in activities that would affect this measure.

Figure 6 shows the five major sources of financial benefit gained from the coaching. Financial benefits gained from improvements in work output constituted 42 percent of the total financial benefit. Retention was the next greatest source of financial benefit, with 29 percent of the total. Increased sales contributed 14 percent of the total, productivity gains contributed 12 percent, and cost reductions contributed 3 percent.

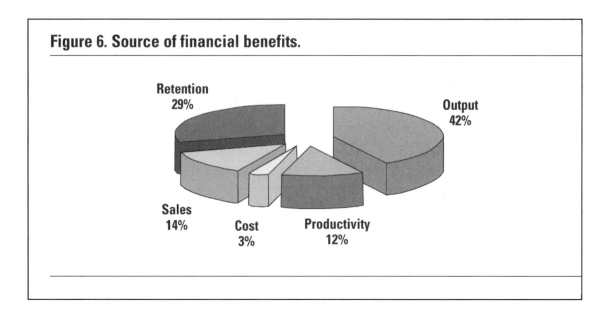

Figure 6. Source of financial benefits.

Level Five: Return-on-Investment

Identifying business impact: Calculations for determining the company's ROI in coaching followed the ROI process developed by Jack Phillips (1997). Following completion of the written survey, the researcher met with each respondent to document the financial benefits of coaching. Each discussion lasted about 20 minutes and focused on areas in which respondents indicated that coaching had a "significant impact" or a "very significant impact" on a key business area. With those who cited tangible financial benefits from coaching, the researcher probed to establish clear links between coaching and changes in client behavior and how this new behavior affected one or more of the business measurement areas. Forty percent of the respondents cited intangible benefits from the coaching but found it difficult to articulate tangible financial benefits. These intangible benefits could not be considered in the final ROI calculation.

Isolating the effects of coaching: Each respondent was asked to estimate the percentage of the benefits attributable to coaching in order to isolate coaching from other factors that could have contributed to the financial benefits. These estimates ranged from 25 percent to 100 percent, averaging 75 percent. Respondents were then asked to estimate their level of confidence in their estimates, which in turn ranged from 30 percent to 100 percent and averaged 69 percent. The financial benefit identified for each respondent was then multiplied by both of these percentage estimates. Therefore, the financial benefits reported in this study are not the total benefits identified by the respondents but rather the benefits that were isolated as due to coaching.

For example, one respondent reported gains in personal productivity measured in terms of hours saved per week. She provided several examples of how, due to coaching, she was able to conduct meetings more efficiently and focus on higher priority work. She estimated a minimum of three to five hours saved per week, 80 percent of which was attributable to coaching. She was 75 percent confident in her estimate, so the benefits were calculated as follows:

3 hours @ $75 = $225 per week * 48 weeks = $10,800 per year

This value was then multiplied by 80 percent (coaching) and 75 percent (confidence) to yield a financial benefit of $6,480.

Determining the ROI: Total program costs were tabulated by Nortel Networks and the Pyramid Resource Group. Costs included the professional fees of the coaches, evaluation costs, time the clients spent being coached, time spent to administer the coaching program and other administrative expense, travel, materials preparation, and all other expenses associated with the coaching program. It should be noted that although the costs of the entire program for 43 clients were included, the benefits were captured from only 30 survey respondents. In other words, the financial benefits from the 30 respondents were spread across the costs generated by 43 coaching clients.

Coaching produced an ROI of 788 percent for Nortel Networks. This was calculated by the following formula (Phillips, 1997):

ROI = [($ Benefits – Program Costs) ÷ Program Costs] x 100

Summary of Intangible Benefits

Although they did not produce tangible financial returns, many benefits cited in this study did create meaningful value for Nortel Networks. For example, significant improvements were made in both employee and customer satisfaction, decision making was improved, and interpersonal relationships and collaboration were enhanced. The coaches reported that their clients developed skills in sizing up situations and more effectively motivating people and leading teams. Almost two-thirds (63 percent) of the respondents reported that coaching accelerated their personal development, improved team performance, and helped them to deal with organizational change. These benefits, although intangible, no doubt contributed in a positive way to the business.

Three-quarters (77 percent) of the respondents thought highly enough of their coaching experiences to recommend coaching to others at Nortel Networks. Those who recommended coaching stressed that, in order to get the most out of coaching, it was important to be open to self-analysis, to look at situations differently, and to try new approaches to address problems. Those who would not recommend coaching complained that the process was too open-ended rather than goal-oriented and that no answers were given by the coaches. Coaching was seen by this group as effective only in dealing with specific situations.

Lessons Learned

The following practices were identified as requirements for the most effective coaching intervention. Many were employed by PRG as a part of Nortel Network's coaching process; some were learned during the process.

- Manage the entire coaching process to ensure consistency and quality. Although the content of individual coaching sessions should always be confidential, the coaching process itself needs to be managed by the client company as well as the coaching company to ensure that the coaching clients and the coaches are following a meaningful process and leveraging client wisdom and best practices. It is critical to have a strong internal contact who works as a partner with the coaching company.

- Prepare clients in advance for coaching and allow it to be a choice. Because coaching remains a relatively new development technique, people may not understand how it can help them become better business professionals. The sooner they understand the process, the sooner they will see results. All potential participants need to attend an orientation session prior to beginning a coaching relationship to really understand the choices they have in the coaching process.

- Offer clients the ability to select their coaches. Chemistry is important to an effective coaching relationship. Provide prospective coaching clients with information about the coaches, including biographies, education, coaching credentials, functional expertise, industry experience, and other background information. Although the coaching company may offer a "best-fit" suggestion, there should be selection options.

- Provide strong organizational support for coaching. Those being coached should receive encouragement and support from their immediate managers. Also, coaching is most effective when conducted in the context of such developmental efforts as competency development, assessments, mentoring, and leadership workshops.

- Ensure that coaches are introduced to the company's business and culture. Coaches are more effective when they can identify with and talk about the realities of their client's environment. Although great coaching is an intuitive process, some background information makes for a fast start.

- Allow each coaching relationship to follow its own path. A major difference between coaching and training is that coaching allows the individual to determine what works best for him or her at a personal level. Coaches need wide latitude to work with "the whole person" and help each client become more effective as a person. This supports clients in becoming more effective as business leaders.

- Build performance measurement into the coaching process. Evaluation of coaching is most reliable when designed into the process from the beginning to better set performance expectations and open up new opportunities to make coaching more effective while it is being conducted. For example, coaching can be refocused to deal with specific problems or to ensure that business priorities will be met. In this way, the evaluation becomes more than just a measuring stick—it becomes a structured approach to deepen the business rationale for coaching.

Questions for Discussion

1. How can you better position coaching with your client or your client's sponsor?

2. What strategies can you use to manage your client's expectations for the financial and intangible value of coaching?

3. How do you link the outcomes of coaching to your client's business objectives?

4. How can integrating measurement with coaching improve the results of coaching?

5. What concerns do you have about entering into conversations with your client about the financial ROI of coaching?

The Authors

Merrill C. Anderson is a business consulting executive, author, and educator with 20 years' experience in improving the performance of people and organizations. He is currently the chief executive officer of MetrixGlobal, a consulting company that provides clients with performance measurement solutions, and a clinical professor in education at Drake University. Anderson earned his doctorate at New York University, his master's degree at the University of Toronto, and his bachelor's degree at the University of Colorado. He can be contacted at merrilland@metrixglobal.net.

Cindy Dauss has been with Nortel Networks since 1980 and has held both management and senior professional positions in a number of diverse areas, including marketing, training and development, human resources, and operations. Dauss was responsible for designing and managing Nortel's Leadership Edge program for the eastern United States and was instrumental in introducing coaching as a key component of the initiative. She has an undergraduate degree from Virginia Tech and a master's in business administration from Duke University's Fuqua School of Business.

Barry F. Mitsch is vice president of the Pyramid Resource Group. He has been involved in training and development activities for nearly 20 years, and his background includes work in both technical and nontechnical training. Mitsch has designed and delivered classroom, self-instructional, and distance learning programs and specializes in group and individual presentation skills training for technical professionals. He can be reached at barry@pyramidresource.com.

References

Kirkpatrick, D.L. (1977). "Evaluating Training Programs: Evidence vs. Proof." *Training & Development,* volume 31, pp. 9-12.

Phillips, J.J. (1997). *Return on Investment in Training and Development Programs.* Boston: Butterworth-Heinemann.

Source: Adapted from D.J. Mitsch, ed. (2002). *In Action: Coaching for Extraordinary Results.* Alexandria, VA: ASTD Press.

Appendix E
Master Reference List

Abernathy, D.J. (August 2001). "Digital Copyrights and Wrongs." *Training & Development*, pp. 27–30.

Albert, B. (1996). *Fat Free Meetings*. Princeton, NJ: Peterson's/Pacesetter.

Allen, M.W. (2003). *Michael Allen's Guide to E-Learning*. Hoboken, NJ: John Wiley & Sons.

Anderson, L.W., et al. (2000). Taxonomy for Learning, Teaching, and Assessing: A Revision of Bloom's Taxonomy of Educational Objectives. New York: Longman.

Argyris, C. (1993). *Knowledge for Action. A Guide to Overcoming Barriers to Organizational Change*. San Francisco: Jossey-Bass.

Arthur, J. (2006). "Countermeasures Matrix." Available at http://www.qimacros.com.

Arthur, M.B., D.T. Hall, and B.S. Lawrence, eds. (1989). *Handbook of Career Theory*. United Kingdom: Cambridge University Press.

Aslanian, C.B., and H.M. Brickell. (1980). *Americans in Transition: Life Changes as Reasons for Adult Learning*. New York: College Entrance Examination Board.

ASTD (American Society for Training & Development). *Evaluating Performance Improvement Interventions*. Version 4. HPI Participant Guide. Alexandria, VA.

———. (2004a). *HPI: Analyzing Human Performance*. HPI Participant Guide. Alexandria, VA.

———. (2004b). *HPI: One-Day Seminar*. HPI Participant Guide. Alexandria, VA.

Averett, P. (Spring 2001). "People: The Human Side of Technology." *The Journal for Quality and Participation*, pp. 34–37.

Barclay, R.O., and P.C. Murray. (1997). "What is Knowledge Management?" *Knowledge Praxis*. Knowledge Management Associates. Available at http://www.media-access.com /whatis.html.

Barksdale, S., and T. Lund. (2001a). *Rapid Evaluation*. Alexandria, VA: ASTD Press.

———. (2001b). *Rapid Needs Analysis*. Alexandria, VA: ASTD Press.

Basarab, D., and D. Root. (1992). *The Training Evaluation Process: A Practical Approach to Evaluating Corporate Training Programs*. New York: Springer.

Beal, T.T. (May 9, 2003). "Simulations on a Shoestring." *Learning Circuits*. Alexandria, VA: ASTD Press.

Beil, D., and M. Kimmel. (1991). "Fundamentals of Quality." *Infoline* No. 259111. (Out of print.)

Bennis, W. (Spring 1999). "The Leadership Advantage." *Leader to Leader,* pp. 18–23.

Bernstein, R., and M. Bergman. (June 18, 2003). "Hispanic Population Reaches All-Time High of 38.8 Million, New Census Bureau Estimates Show." U.S. Census Bureau/United States Department of Commerce. Available at http://www.census .gov/Press Release/www/2003/cb03-100.html.

Bernthal, P.R., et al. (2004). *The ASTD Competency Study: Mapping the Future.* Alexandria, VA: ASTD Press.

Berryman-Find, C., and C.B. Fink. (1996). *The Manager's Desk Reference.* 2nd edition. New York: AMACOM.

Biech, E. (2005). *Training for Dummies®.* Hoboken, NJ: Wiley Publishing.

Biech, E., and M. Danahy. (1991). "Diagnostic Tools for Total Quality." *Infoline* No. 259109. (Out of print.)

Bierema, L.L. (2002). "The Sociocultural Contexts of Learning in the Workplace." In M.V. Alfred, ed., *Learning and Sociocultural Contexts: Implications for Adults, Community, and Workplace Education.* San Francisco: Jossey-Bass, pp. 69–78.

Bloom, B., T. Hastings, and G.F. Madaus. (1971). *Handbook of Formative and Summative Evaluation of Student Learning.* New York: McGraw-Hill.

Bluman, A.G. (2003). *Elementary Statistics: A Step by Step Approach.* 2nd edition. New York: McGraw-Hill.

Bonk, C.J. (November 2002). "Collaborative Tools for E-Learning." *Chief Learning Officer: Solutions for Enterprise Productivity.* Available at http://www.clomedia.com /content/templates/clo_feature.asp?articleid=41&zoneid=30.

Borisoff, D., and D.A. Victor. (1989). *Conflict Management: A Communication Skills Approach.* Englewood Cliffs, NJ: Prentice-Hall.

Branham, L. (2001). *Keeping the People Who Keep You in Business.* New York: AMACOM.

Bridges, W. (1980). *Transitions.* Reading, MA: Addison-Wesley.

Briggs, K.C., and I.B. Myers. (1977). *Myers-Briggs Type Indicator.* Palo Alto, CA: Consulting Psychologists Press.

Brim, O.G. (1968). "Adult Socialization and Society." In J. Clausen, ed., *Socialization and Society.* Boston: Little, Brown.

Brim, O.G., and C.D. Ryff. (1980). "On the Properties of Life Events." In R. Baltes and O.G. Brim, eds., *Life-Span Development and Behavior.* Volume 3. New York: Academic Press.

Brinkerhoff, R. (1998). *Moving From Training to Performance.* Alexandria, VA: ASTD.

Brogden, H.E. (1946). "On the Interpretation of the Correlation Coefficient as a Measure of Predictive Efficiency." *Journal of Educational Psychology,* pp. 37, 65-76.

Brookfield, D. (1986). *Understanding and Facilitating Adult Learning.* San Francisco: Jossey-Bass.

Brookfield, S. (1987). *Developing Critical Thinkers.* San Francisco: Jossey-Bass.

Bruce, A. (2001). *Leaders—Start to Finish.* Alexandria, VA: ASTD Press.

Buckner, M. (1999). "Simulation and Role Play." *Infoline* No. 258412.

Buckner, M., and L. Slavenski. (1993). "Succession Planning." *Infoline* No. 259312.

Butler, S. (September 1999). "Knowledge Management Directions: Database Management Considerations for BI and KM." Available at: http://dmreview.com /article_sub.cfm?articleId=1355.

Butruille, S. (1988). "Listening to Learn; Learning to Listen." *Infoline* No. 258806.

———. (1989). "Lesson Design and Development." *Infoline* No. 258906.

Cadzow, L., and P. Lake. (2002). "Drive Change With Case Studies." *Infoline* No. 250211.

Callahan, M., ed. (1985). "Business Basics." *Infoline* No. 258511. (Out of print.)

Canfield, A.A. (1988). *Canfield Learning Styles Inventory (LSI).* Los Angeles: Western Psychological Services.

Carliner, S. (1995). *Every Object Tells a Story: A Grounded Model of Design for Object-Based Learning in Museums.* Doctoral dissertation. Atlanta, GA: Georgia State University.

———. (2002). *Designing E-Learning.* Alexandria, VA: ASTD Press.

———. (2003). *Training Design Basics.* Alexandria, VA: ASTD Press.

———. (November 2005). "Course Management Systems Versus Learning Management Systems." *Learning Circuits.* Available at http://www.learningcircuits.org/2005 /nov2005/carliner.html.

Carnegie Mellon Software Engineering Institute. (2005). "Six Sigma: Software Technology Roadmap." Available at http://www.sei.cmu.edu/str/descriptions/sigma6 _body.html.

Carr, D.A. (1994). "How to Facilitate." *Infoline* No. 259406.

Carter, R.T., ed. (2004). *Addressing Cultural Issues in Organizations.* London: Sage.

Caudron, S. (October 21, 1996). "Hire a Coach?" *Industry Week,* pp. 87-91.

Chapple, M. (October 2004). "Database Fundamentals." Available at http://databases.about.com/od/administration/a/databasefund.htm.

———. "Choosing a Database Product." Available at http://databases .about.com/od/administration/a/choosing.htm.

Cheney, S. (1998). "Benchmarking." *Infoline* No. 259801.

Cherniss, C., and M. Adler. (2000). *Promoting Emotional Intelligence in Organizations.* Alexandria, VA: ASTD Press.

Clark, D. (1999). "A Time Capsule of Learning and Training." Available at http://www.nwlink.com/~donclark/hrd/history/knowledge.html.

Conkright, T.D. (January 1988). "So You're Going to Manage a Project...." *Training*, pp. 62–67.

Connor, D. (1992). *Managing at the Speed of Change*. New York: Villard Books.

Conover, D.K. (1996). "Leadership Development." In R.L Craig, ed., *The ASTD Training and Development Handbook*. 4th edition. New York: McGraw-Hill.

Conway, M. (1998). "How to Collect Data." *Infoline* No. 259008. (Out of print.)

————. (2004). "Collecting Data With Electronic Tools." *Infoline* No. 250404.

Conway, M., and M. Cassidy. (2001). "Evaluating Trainer Effectiveness." *Infoline* No. 250103.

Conway, M., and S. Thomas. (2003). "Using Electronic Surveys." *Infoline* No. 250301.

Cooperrider, D., D. Whitney, and J. Stavros. (2003). *Appreciative Inquiry Handbook: The First in a Series of AI Workbooks for Leaders of Change*. Brunswick, OH: Lakeshore Communications.

Couris, J., C. Zulauf, and C. Kennedy. (2000). *Best Practices in Knowledge Management and Organizational Learning Handbook*. Burlington, MA: Linkage.

Cowan, S.L. (1999). "Change Management." *Infoline* No. 259904.

————. (2000). "Outsourcing Training." *Infoline* No. 250002.

Craig, R.L., ed. (1996). *The ASTD Training and Development Handbook*. 4th edition. New York: McGraw-Hill.

Cross, P. (1981). *Adults as Learners: Increasing Participation and Facilitating Learning*. San Francisco: Jossey-Bass.

Cross, R., and L. Baird. (Spring 2000). "Technology is Not Enough: Improving Performance by Building Organizational Memory." *Sloan Management Review*. pp.69–78.

Daloz, L.A. (1986). *Effective Teaching and Mentoring: Realizing the Transformational Power of Adult Learning Experiences*. San Francisco: Jossey-Bass.

Darraugh, B. (1990a). "Coaching and Feedback." *Infoline* No. 259006.

————. (1990b). "How to Survive Mergers and Downsizings." *Infoline* No. 259010.

————. (1992). "How to Build a Successful Team." *Infoline* No. 259212. (Out of print.)

————. (1993). "Understanding Reengineering: Organizational Transformation." *Infoline* No. 259308.

————. (1997). "How to Motivate Employees." *Infoline* No. 259108. (Out of print.)

Davenport, T.H., and L. Prusak. (1998). *Working Knowledge*. Boston: Harvard Business School Press.

Dearden, J. (1999). "Evaluating Off-the-Shelf CBT Courseware." *Infoline* No. 259908.

DeLisi, P.S. (Fall 1990). "Lessons From the Steel Axe: Culture, Technology, and Organizational Change." *Sloan Management Review*, pp. 83–93.

Denison, D. (Spring 1984). "Bringing Corporate Culture to the Bottom Line." *Organizational Dynamics,* pp. 4–22.

———. (Fall 1996). "What Is the Difference Between Organizational Culture and Organizational Climate: A Native's Point of View on a Decade of Paradigm Wars." *Academy of Management Review*, pp. 619-654.

Dent, J., and P. Anderson. (1998). "Fundamentals of HPI." *Infoline* No. 259811.

DeRose, G.J. (1999). *Outsourcing Training and Education.* Alexandria, VA: ASTD Press.

Dick, W.O., and L. Carey. (1996). *The Systematic Design of Instruction.* 3rd edition. New York: HarperCollins College.

Dick, W.O., L. Carey, and J.O. Carey. (2004). *The Systematic Design of Instruction.* 6th edition. Boston: Allyn & Bacon.

Digh, P. (1998). "Race Matters." *Mosaics: Society of Human Performance Development*, pp. 1ff.

Duncan, W.R. (1996). *A Guide to the Project Management Body of Knowledge.* Newton Square, PA: Project Management Institute.

Dunn, R., et al. (1982). *Productivity Environmental Preference Survey.* Lawrence, KS: Price Systems.

Durrance, B. (April 1997). "The Evolutionary Vision of Dee Hock." *Training & Development,* pp. 24-31.

Eitington, J.E. (2002). *The Winning Trainer: Winning Ways to Involve People in Learning.* Woburn, MA: Butterworth-Heinemann.

Elengold, L.J. (2001). "Teach SMEs to Design Training." *Infoline* No. 250106.

Ellis, A.L., E.D. Wagner, and W.R. Longmire. (1999). *Managing Web-Based Training.* Alexandria, VA: ASTD Press.

Ellis, Ryann K. (December 15, 2005). "Virtual Schools Get a Lift from BellSouth Corp." *Learning Circuits.* Available at http://www.learningcircuits.org.

Elsenheimer, J. (February 2003). "Terms of Engagement: Keeping Learners Online." *Learning Circuits.* Available at: http://www.learningcircuits.org.

Estep, T. (2004). "Organization Development for Trainers." *Infoline* No. 250411.

———. (2005). "Meetings That Work!" *Infoline* No. 250505.

Evans, K., and D. Metzger. (2000). "Storytelling." *Infoline* No. 250006.

Eyers, P.S. (1996). "Training and the Law." In R.L. Craig, ed., *The ASTD Training and Development Handbook.* 4th edition. New York: McGraw-Hill.

Fairbanks, D.M. (1992). "Accelerated Learning." *Infoline* No. 259209.

Finkel, C., and A.D. Finkel. (2000). "Facilities Planning." *Infoline* No. 258504.

Finn, T. (1999). "Valuing and Managing Diversity." *Infoline* No. 259305.

Finnerty, M.F. (1996). "Coaching for Growth and Development." In R.L. Craig, ed., *The ASTD Training & Development Handbook.* 4th edition. New York: McGraw-Hill.

Fitz-enz, J. (2000). *The ROI of Human Capital: Measuring the Economic Value of Employee Performance.* New York: AMACOM.

Forbess-Greene, S. (1983). *The Encyclopedia of Icebreakers.* New York: John Wiley & Sons.

Fort, L. (2005). "Foundations of Six Sigma: Customer and Process." In *Six Sigma in Transactional and Service Environments.* Available at http://www.fassbex.com/articles /145.

Fournies, F.F. (1987). *Coaching for Improved Work Performance.* New York: Liberty Hall Press.

Francis, L. (September 2001). "Expect More From E-Learning." *Learning Circuits.* Available at http://www.learningcircuits.org.

Frankel, L.P., and K.L. Otzao. (Autumn 1992). "Employee Coaching: The Way to Gain Commitment, Not Just Compliance." *Employee Relations Today,* pp. 311-320.

Franklin, M. (2005). "A Guide to Job Analysis." *Infoline* No. 250506.

Gagne, R.M., L.J. Briggs, and W.W. Wager. (1988). *Principles of Instructional Design.* 3rd edition. New York: Holt, Rinehart, and Winston.

GAO (U.S. General Accountability Office). (2001). "Older Workers: Demographic Trends Pose Challenges for Employers and Workers." Washington, D.C. Available at http://www.gap.gov/new.items/d0285.pdf.

————. (February 1992). Organizational Culture: Techniques Companies Use to Perpetuate or Change Beliefs and Values. GAO/NSIAD-92-105. Washington, D.C.

Gardner, H. (1983). *Frames of Mind: The Theory of Multiple Intelligences.* New York: Basic Books.

Garrett, J.J. (2002). "A Visual Vocabulary for Describing Information Architecture and Interaction Design." Available at http://www.jjg.net/ia/visvocab/.

Gibson, R.S. (1998). "Selecting a Coach." *Infoline* No. 259812.

Gilbert, T. (1978). *Human Competence: Engineering Worthy Performance.* New York: McGraw-Hill.

————. (October 1982). "A Question of Performance—Part II: The PROBE Model." *Training & Development,* pp. 85–89.

————. (September 1982). "A Question of Performance—Part I: The PROBE Model." *Training & Development,* pp. 20–30.

————. (1996). *Human Competence: Engineering Worthy Performance.* ISPI Tribute edition. Washington, DC: International Society for Performance Improvement/Amherst, MA: HRD Press.

Gillespie Myers, J. (2005). "How to Select and Use Learning Tools." *Infoline* No. 250507.

Gilley, J.W. (1992). "Strategic Planning for Human Resource Development." *Infoline* No. 259206. (Out of print.)

Goldsmith, J.J. (2000). "Development Teams for Creating Technology-Based Training." In G. Piskurich, P. Beckschi, and B. Hall, eds., *The ASTD Handbook of Training Design and Delivery.* New York: McGraw-Hill.

Goldsmith, M., et al. (2003). *Global Leadership: The Next Generation.* Upper Saddle River, NJ: Pearson Education.

Gordon, E.E., and J.E. Baumhart. (1995). "Ethics for Training and Development." *Infoline* No. 259515. (Out of print.)

Grant, E.L., and R.S. Leavenworth. (1996). *Statistical Quality Control.* 7th edition. New York: McGraw-Hill

Gray, C. (1998). *Enterprise and Culture.* London: Routledge.

Greenberg, L. (December 2002). "LMS and LCMS: What's the Difference?" *Learning Circuits.* Available at http://www.learningcircuits.org.

Groff, T.R., and T.P. Jones. (2003). *Introduction to Knowledge Management.* Burlington, MA: Butterworth-Heinemann.

Guillot, T. (2002). "Team Building in a Virtual Environment." *Infoline* No. 250205.

Guss, E. (2005). "Emotional Intelligence: Our Most Versatile Tool for Success." ASTD white paper. Available at http://www.astd.org/astd/Publications/Whitepapers /Emot_Intel+Dec_05.htm.

Hackman, J.R., and G.R. Oldham. (1975). "Development of the Job Diagnostic Survey." *Journal of Applied Psychology*, pp. 159–170.

Hall, E.T. (1969). *The Hidden Dimension.* Garden City, NJ: McGraw-Hill.

————. (1977). *Beyond Culture.* New York: Anchor Books.

Hall, S.O., and B. Hall. (November 2004). "A Guide to Learning Content Management Systems." *Training*, pp. 33–37.

Hambrick, D., D. Nadler, and M. Tushman. (1998). *Navigating Change.* Boston: Harvard Business School Press.

Haneberg, L. (2005a). *Coaching Basics.* Alexandria, VA: ASTD Press.

————. (2005b). *Organization Development Basics.* Alexandria, VA: ASTD Press.

Hargrove, R. (1995). *Masterful Coaching: Extraordinary Results by Impacting People and the Way They Think and Work Together.* San Diego: Pfeiffer.

Harris, J., and S. Hartman. (2002). *Organizational Behavior.* Binghamton, NY: Best Business Books.

Harris, P.M., and O.S. Castillo. (2002). "Instructional Design for WBT." *Infoline* No. 250202.

Hartley, D.E. (September 2004). "Job Analysis at the Speed of Reality." *T+D,* pp. 20-22.

Hastings, S. (2004). "Succession Planning: Take Two." *Infoline* No. 250405.

Herriot, P., and R. Strickland, ed. (1997). "The Management of Careers." Special issue. *European Journal of Work and Organizational Psychology,* 5(4).

Herrmann, N. (1988). *The Creative Brain.* Lake Lure, NC: Brain Books.

————. (1989). *The Creative Brain.* Revised edition. Lake Lure, NC: Brain Books.

Herschbach, D.R. (Spring 1992). "Technology and Efficiency: Competencies as Content." *Journal of Technology Education* 3 (2), pp. 15-25.

Herzberg, F. (1966). *Work and the Nature of Man.* Cleveland: The World Publishing Company.

Hiemstra, R. (1993). "Three Underdeveloped Models for Adult Learning." Available at http://home.twcny.rr.com/hiemstra/ndacesm.html.

Hodell, C. (1997). "Basics of Instructional Systems Development." *Infoline* No. 259706.

————. (1999). "Lesson Design and Development." *Infoline* No. 258906.

————. (2000). *ISD From the Ground Up.* Alexandria, VA: ASTD Press.

Honey, P., and A. Mumford. (1989). *Learning Styles Questionnaire.* King of Prussia, PA: Organization Development and Design.

Horton, W. (2002). *Using E-Learning.* Alexandria, VA: ASTD Press.

Howard, A.H. (1996). "Apprenticeship." In R.L. Craig, ed., *The ASTD Training and Development Handbook.* 4th edition. Alexandria, VA: ASTD Press.

Hultsch, D.F., and J.K. Plemons. (1979). "Life Events and Life Span Development." In P. Baltes and O.G. Brim, eds., *Life-Span Development and Behavior.* Volume 2. New York: Academic Press.

Jacobsen, S. (1994). "Neurolinguistic Programming." *Infoline* No. 259404. (Out of print.)

James, W.B., and M.W. Galbraith. (1985). "Perceptual Learning Styles: Implications and Techniques for the Practitioner." *Lifelong Learning,* pp. 20–23.

Jarvis, P. (1987). *Adult Learning in the Social Context.* London: Croom Helm.

Jarvis, P., J. Holford, and C. Griffin. (2003) *The Theory and Practice of Learning.* Oxford, United Kingdom: Routledge Taylor and Francis and Group.

Jennings, J., and L. Malcak. (2004). *Communication Basics.* Alexandria, VA: ASTD Press.

Johnson, D., et al. (2005). *Joining Together: Group Theory and Group Skills.* 5th edition. Boston: Allyn & Bacon.

Johnson, G. (October 2004). "The Perfect Storm." *Training*, pp. 38–49.

Johnson, J. (2004). "Ethics for Trainers." *Infoline* No. 250406.

Jorz, J., and L. Oliver. (1985). "How to Create a Good Learning Environment." *Infoline* No. 258506.

Juran, J. (1964). *Managerial Breakthrough: A New Concept of the Manager's Job.* New York: McGraw-Hill.

Kamine, M., C. de Mello-e-Souza Wildermuth, and R. Collins. (2003). "Diversity Programs That Work." *Infoline* No. 250312.

Kamphaus, R.W., and C.R. Reynolds, eds. (1990). *Handbook of Psychological and Educational Assessment of Children.* New York: Guilford Press.

Kaplan, R., and D. Norton. (1996). *The Balanced Scorecard.* Boston: Harvard Business Press.

Karmlinger, T., and T. Huberty. (December 1990). "Behaviorism Versus Humanism." *Training & Development,* pp. 41–45.

Kauffman, D.L. (1980). *Systems 1: An Introduction to Systems Thinking.* Minneapolis, MN: Future Systems.

Kaye, B., and D. Scheef. (2000). "Mentoring." *Infoline* No. 250004.

Kaye, B.L., and S. Jordan-Evans. (December 2000). "The ABCs of Management Gift-Giving." *Training & Development,* pp. 51-54.

Kearsley, G. (1982). *Cost, Benefits, & Productivity in Training Systems.* Boston: Addison-Wesley.

Kepner, C.H., and B.B. Tregoe. (1981). *The New Rational Manager.* Princeton, NJ: Princeton Research Press.

Kim, D. (1992). *Systems Archetypes I: Diagnosing Systemic Issues and Designing High-Leverage Interventions.* Cambridge, MA: Pegasus.

————. (1994). *Systems Archetypes II: Using Systems Archetypes to Take Effective Action.* Cambridge, MA: Pegasus.

Kirkpatrick, D.L. (1977). "Evaluating Training Programs: Evidence vs. Proof." *Training & Development,* volume 31, pp. 9-12.

————. (1994). *Evaluating Training Programs.* San Francisco, CA: Berrett-Koehler.

————. (1998a). *Evaluating Training Programs: The Four Levels.* 2nd edition. San Francisco, CA: Berrett-Koehler.

————. (1998b). Another Look at Evaluating Training Programs. Alexandria, VA: ASTD Press.

Kirrane, D. (1988). "Listening to Learn: Learning to Listen." *Infoline* No. 258806. (Out of print.)

Knowles, M. (1984). *The Adult Learner: A Neglected Species.* 3rd edition. Houston, TX: Gulf Publishing.

Knowles, M. (1988). *The Modern Practice of Adult Education: From Pedagogy to Andragogy.* Cambridge, MA. Cambridge Book Company.

Knowles, M.S., E.F. Holton, and R.A. Swanson. (2005). *The Adult Learner.* Burlington, MA: Elsevier/Butterworth Heinemann.

Koehle, D. (1997). "The Role of the Performance Change Manager." *Infoline* No. 259715.

Kolb, D.A. (1984). *Experiential Learning: Experience as the Source of Learning and Development.* Englewood Cliffs, NJ: Prentice-Hall.

Kotter, J.P. (1996). *Leading Change.* Boston: Harvard Business School Press.

Kristiansen, N.S. (2004). "Making Smile Sheets Count." *Infoline* No. 250402.

Lambert, C. (1986). *Secrets of a Successful Trainer.* New York: John Wiley & Sons. (Out of print.)

Langer, A.M. (2001). *Analysis and Design of Information Systems,* 2nd edition. New York: Springer-Verlag.

Larsen, N.G. (2002). "Implementing Strategic Learning." *Infoline* No. 250210.

Lauby, S. (2005). "Motivating Employees." *Infoline* No. 250510.

Lawson, K. (1997). *Improving On-the-Job Training and Coaching.* Alexandria, VA: ASTD Press.

Lazanov, G. (1981). *Suggestology and Outlines of Suggestopedia.* New York: Gordon & Breach.

Lee, A.Y., and A.N. Bowers. (1997). "The Effects of Multimedia Components on Learning." Proceedings of the Human Factors and Ergonomics Society 41st Annual Meeting, pp. 340–344.

Leibowitz, Z.B. (1986). *Designing Career Development Systems.* San Francisco: Jossey-Bass.

Leibowitz, Z.B., A.H. Souerwine, and J.E. McMahon. (1985). "Career Guidance Discussions." *Infoline* No. 258507.

Leiper, R. (2004). *The Psychodynamic Approach.* London: Sage.

Livingston, J.S. (September 2002). "Pygmalion in Management." *Harvard Business Review,* pp. 81–89.

Long, L. (1986). "Surveys From Start to Finish." *Infoline* No. 258612.

———. (2003). "Harness the Power of Coaching." *Infoline* No. 250310.

Lyerly, B., and C. Maxey. (2000). *Training From the Heart.* Alexandria, VA: ASTD Press.

Lyons, D.J., et al. (1985). "Business Basics." *Infoline* No. 258511. (Out of print.)

Mager, R.F. (1962). Preparing Objectives for Programmed Instruction. Palo Alto, CA: Fearon.

Magruder Watkins, J., and B.J. Mohr. (2001). *Appreciative Inquiry: Change at the Speed of Imagination.* San Francisco: Jossey-Bass/Pfeiffer.

Mantyla, K. (2001). *Blended E-Learning.* Alexandria, VA: ASTD Press.

Mantyla, K., and J.R. Gividen. (1997). *Distance Learning: A Step-by-Step Guide for Trainers.* Alexandria, VA: ASTD Press.

Maresh, N. (2000). "Breathing Life Into Adult Learning." In G. Piskurich, P. Beckschi, and B. Hall, eds., *The ASTD Handbook of Training Design and Delivery.* New York: McGraw-Hill.

Marquardt, M. (1996). *Building the Learning Organization.* New York: McGraw-Hill.

————. (1997). "Action Learning." *Infoline* No. 259704.

————. (1999). "Successful Global Training." *Infoline* No. 259913.

————. (1999). *Action Learning in Action.* Palo Alto, CA: Davies-Black Publishing.

————. (2004). *Optimizing the Power of Action Learning.* Palo Alto, CA: Davies-Black Publishing.

Marshall, V., and R. Schriver. (January 1994). "Using Evaluation to Improve Performance." *Technical and Skills Training,* pp. 6-9.

Martelli, J.T., and D. Mathern. (1991). "Statistics for HRD Practice." *Infoline* No. 259101.

Marx, R.J. (1999). *The ASTD Media Selection Tool for Training and Performance Improvement.* Alexandria, VA: ASTD Press. (Out of print.)

Maslow, A. (1954). *Motivation and Personality.* New York: Harper.

Maurer, T.J., and N.E. Rafuse. (2001). "Learning, not Litigating: Managing Employee Development and Avoiding Claims of Age Discrimination." *Academy of Management Executive,* pp. 110–121.

Mayer, J.D., P. Salovey, and D. Caruso. (1998). "Competing Models of Emotional Intelligence." In R.J. Steinberg, ed., *Handbook of Human Intelligence,* New York: Cambridge University Press.

McArdle, G.E. (1993). *Delivering Effective Training Sessions.* Menlo Park, CA: Crisp Publications.

————. (1999). *Training Design and Delivery.* Alexandria, VA: ASTD Press.

McBrien, K. (May 2005). "Developing Localization Friendly E-Learning." *Learning Circuits.* Available at http://www.learningcircuits.org.

McCain, D.V. (2005). *Evaluation Basics.* Alexandria, VA: ASTD Press.

McClanaghan, M. (2000). "A Strategy for Helping Students Learn How to Learn." *Education,* pp. 479–486.

McGregor, D. (1960). *The Human Side of Enterprise.* New York: McGraw-Hill.

McLagan, P. (1989). *Models for HRD Practice.* Alexandria, VA: ASTD. (Out of print.)

McMurrer, D., M.E. Van Buren, and W. Woodwell. (2000). *The 2000 ASTD State of the Industry Report.* Alexandria, VA: ASTD.

Merriam, S.B. (1984). *Adult Development: Implications for Adult Education.* Columbus, OH: ERIC Clearinghouse on Adult, Career, and Vocational Education.

Merriam, S.B., and R.S. Caffarella. (1991). *Learning in Adulthood.* San Francisco: Jossey-Bass.

Metcalf, D.S. II. (2000). "Using Audio and Video Over the Web." In G. Piskurich, P. Beckschi, and B. Hall, eds., *The ASTD Handbook of Training Design and Delivery.* New York: McGraw-Hill.

Millward, L. (2005). *Understanding Occupational & Organizational Psychology.* London: Sage Publications.

Miner, N. (2001). "The One-Person Training Department." *Infoline* No. 250107 (Out of print.)

Mink, O.G., K.Q. Owen, and B.P. Mink. (1996). *Developing High-Performance People: The Art of Coaching.* Reading, MA: Addison-Wesley.

Mische, M. (2001). *Strategic Renewal.* Upper Saddle River, NJ: Prentice-Hall.

Mitchell, L. (1996). *Peterson's The Ultimate Grad School Survival Guide.* Lawrenceville, NJ: Thompson Peterson's.

Modell, M.E. (1996). *A Professional's Guide to Systems Analysis.* New York: McGraw-Hill.

Mohn, C.G., S. Field, and G. Frank. (2000). "Virtual Reality: Is It for You?" In G. Piskurich, P. Beckschi, and B. Hall, eds., *The ASTD Handbook of Training Design and Delivery.* New York: McGraw-Hill.

Moran, J.V. (January 2002). "Mission: Buy an LMS." *Learning Circuits.* Available at http://www.learningcircuits.org.

Morris, B. (February 2000). "Executive Coaches: So You're a Player: Do You Need a Coach?" *Fortune,* p. 144.

Moss Kanter, R. (1985). *The Change Masters: Innovation and Entrepreneurship in the American Corporation.* New York: Simon & Schuster.

Mulcahy Boer, P. (2001). *Career Counseling Over the Internet: An Emerging Model for Trusting and Responding to Online Clients.* Mahwah, NJ: Lawrence Erlbaum Associates.

Munro, R., and E. Rice. (1993). "The Malcolm Baldrige National Quality Award and Trainers." *Infoline* No. 259302. (Out of print.)

Murrell, K. (1993). "Organizational Culture." *Infoline* No. 259304.

Myers, I.B., and M.H. Mcaulley. (1985). *Manual: A Guide to the Development of the Myers-Briggs Type Indicator.* Palo Alto, CA: Consulting Psychologists Press.

Myers, S. (1990). "Basics of Intercultural Communication." *Infoline* No. 259009. (Out of print.)

Nadler, L. (1994). *Designing Training Programs.* 2nd edition. Houston, TX: Gulf Publishing.

National Career Development Association. (1997). "Career Counseling Competencies." Available at http://www.ncda.org/pdf/counselingcompetencies.pdf.

National Institute of Open Schooling. (Accessed February 2006). "Lesson 29: Introduction to System Design and Analysis." Available at http://www.nos.org/htm/sad1.htm.

Nelson, B. (1994). *1001 Ways to Reward Employees.* New York: Workman Publishing.

Neugarten, B. (1976). "Adaptation and the Life Cycle." *Counseling Psychologist,* 6, pp. 16-20.

————. (1979). "Time, Age, and the Life Cycle." *American Journal of Psychiatry,* pp. 136, 887-893.

Neugarten, B., and N. Datan. (1973). "Sociological Perspectives on the Life Cycle." In P. Baltes and K.W. Schaie, eds., *Life-Span Development Psychology: Personality and Socialization.* New York: Academic Press.

Newman, A. (1999). "Knowledge Management." *Infoline* No. 259903.

Nilson, C. (1999). *How to Start a Training Program.* Alexandria, VA: ASTD Press.

Nonaka, I., and H. Takeuchi. (1995). *The Knowledge-Creating Company.* New York: Oxford University Press.

Novak, C. (1997). "High Performance Training Manuals." *Infoline* No. 259707. (Out of print.)

O'Keefe, C. (June 2005). "How to Create an Environment for Successful Change." *OD Leadership Network News,* Available at http://www.astd.org/astd /publications/newsletters/od_leadership_news.

Oakes, K., and R. Rengarajan. (September 2002). "E-Learning: Synching Up With Virtual Classrooms." *T&D,* pp. 57–60.

Oberstein, S., and J. Alleman. (2003). *Beyond Free Coffee and Donuts.* Alexandria, VA: ASTD Press.

Osipow, S.H., and W.B. Walsh. (1988). *Career Decision Making.* Mahwah, NJ: Laurence Earlbaum Associates.

Patterson, J.G. (1994). "Fundamentals of Leadership." *Infoline* No. 259402. (Out of print.)

Peters, T., and N. Austin. (1984). *A Passion for Excellence.* New York: Random House.

Pfeiffer, W., and J.E. Jones. (1975). *A Handbook of Structured Experiences for Human Relations Training.* Volumes 1-5. La Jolla, CA: University Associates.

Phillips, J.J. (1997a). *Return on Investment in Training and Development Programs.* Boston: Butterworth-Heinemann.

————. (1997b). *In Action: Leading Organizational Change.* Alexandria, VA: ASTD Press.

————. (1998a). "Level 1 Evaluation: Reaction and Planned Action." *Infoline* No. 259813.

————. (1998b). "Level 2 Evaluation: Learning." *Infoline* No. 259814.

————. (1998c). "Level 3 Evaluation: Application." *Infoline* No. 259815.

————. (2002). *In Action: Retaining Your Best Employees.* Alexandria, VA: ASTD Press.

————. (2005). *Investing in Your Company's Human Capital.* New York: AMACOM.

Phillips, J.J., P.P. Phillips, and T. Hodges. (2004). *Make Training Evaluation Work.* Alexandria, VA: ASTD Press.

Phillips, J.J., P.P. Phillips, and W. Wurtz. (1998). "Level 5 Evaluation: Mastering ROI." *Infoline* No. 259805.

Phillips, P.P., C. Gaudet, and J.J. Phillips. (2003). "Evaluation Data: Planning and Use." *Infoline* No. 250304.

Pietrzak, T. (2005). "Building Career Success Skills." *Infoline* No. 250501.

Piskurich, G. (2000). "Make It Easier for Them to Learn on Their Own: Instructional Design for Technology-Based, Self-Instructional Applications." In Piskurich, G., P. Beckschi, and B. Hall, eds., *The ASTD Handbook of Training Design and Delivery.* New York: McGraw-Hill.

————. (2001). "Facilitating Synchronous WBT." *Infoline* No. 250112.

————. (2002). *HPI Essentials.* Alexandria, VA: ASTD Press.

————. (2003). *Trainer Basics.* Alexandria, VA: ASTD Press.

Piskurich, G., and E.S. Sanders. (1998). *ASTD Models for Learning Technologies: Roles, Competencies, and Outputs.* Alexandria, VA: ASTD Press.

Piskurich, G., P. Beckschi, and B. Hall, eds. (2000). *The ASTD Handbook of Training Design and Delivery.* New York: McGraw-Hill.

Plattner, F.B. (1994). "Improve Your Communication and Speaking Skills." *Infoline* No. 259409.

Pope-Davis, D.B., et al. (2003). *Handbook of Multicultural Competencies.* United Kingdom: Sage.

Popham, W.J. (1973). *Educational Statistics: Use and Interpretation.* New York: Harper and Row.

Prezioso, R.C. (1998). "Icebreakers." *Infoline* No. 258911.

Price, J., and L. Price. (2002). *Hot Text: Web Writing That Works.* Indianapolis: New Riders.

Prochaska, J.O., J. Norcross, and C. DiClemente. (1994). *Changing for Good.* New York: William Morrow and Company.

Quick, T.L. (1985). *The Manager's Motivation Desk Book.* New York: John Wiley and Sons.

Quinlivan-Hall, D., and P. Renner. (1990). *In Search of Solutions.* Vancouver, BC: PFR Training Associates.

Reio, T.G., and J. Saunders-Reio. (1999). "Combating Workplace Ageism." *Adult Learning,* pp. 10–13.

Renfrew, Paul. (2002). "IPO." Available at http://www.isixsigma.com/dictionary/I-P-O-491.htm.

Revans, R. (1982). "What Is Action Learning?" *Journal of Management Development,* pp. 64–75.

Reynolds, A. (1993). *The Trainer's Dictionary: HRD Terms, Acronyms, Initials, and Abbreviations.* Amherst, MA: HRD Press.

Rhinesmith, S.H. (1996). "Training for Global Operations." In R.L. Craig, ed. *The ASTD Training and Development Handbook.* 4th edition. New York: McGraw-Hill.

Robbins, H.A. (1992). *How to Speak and Listen Effectively.* New York, NY: AMACOM.

Robertson, J. (January 2002). "How to Evaluate a Content Management System." KM Column. Available at: http://www.steptwo.com.au/papers/kmc_evaluate/pdf/KMC_EvaluateCMS.pdf.

Roos, J. (February 1997). "The Poised Organization: Navigating Effectively on Knowledge Landscapes." *The Strategy & Complexity Seminal.* London: London School of Economics.

Roper Starch Worldwide. (February 1999). "Baby Boomers Envision Their Retirement: An AARP Segmentation Analysis." American Association of Retired Persons. Available at http://research.aarp.org/econ/boomer_seg.html.

Rosania, R.J. (2003). *Presentation Basics.* Alexandria, VA: ASTD Press.

Rose, E., and S. Buckley. (1999). *Self-Directed Work Teams.* Alexandria, VA: ASTD Press.

Rosen, S., and C. Paul. (1997). *Career Renewal.* San Diego, CA: Academic Press.

Rosenberg, M.J. (1996). "Human Performance Technology." In R.L. Craig, ed., *The ASTD Training and Development Handbook.* 4th edition. New York: McGraw-Hill.

Rosenberg, M.J. (2001). *E-Learning: Strategies for Delivering Knowledge in the Digital Age.* New York: McGraw-Hill.

Rossen, E., and D. Hartley. (2001). "Basics of E-Learning." *Infoline* No. 250109.

Rossett, A. (1987). *Training Needs Assessment: Techniques in Training and Performance.* Englewood Cliffs, NJ: Education Technology Publications.

———. (1992). "Analysis of Human Performance Problems." In H.D. Stolovitch and E.J. Keeps, eds., *Handbook of Human Performance Technology: A Comprehensive Guide for Analyzing and Solving Performance Problems.* San Francisco: Jossey-Bass.

Rothwell, W.J. (1996a). "Selecting and Developing the Professional Human Resource Staff." In Robert L. Craig, ed., *The ASTD Training and Development Handbook*. New York: McGraw-Hill.

————. (1996b). *ASTD Models for Human Performance Improvement*. Alexandria, VA: ASTD Press.

————. (2000). *Effective Succession Planning*. 2nd edition. New York: AMACOM.

Rothwell, W.J., et al. (1999). *ASTD Models for Workplace Learning and Performance: Roles, Competencies, and Outputs*. Alexandria, VA: ASTD Press.

Rumizen, M. (2002). *The Complete Idiot's Guide to Knowledge Management*. Madison, WI: CWL Publishing.

Rummler, G., and A. Brache. (1995). *Improving Performance: How to Manage the White Space on the Organization Chart*. 2nd edition. San Francisco: Jossey-Bass.

Rumsey, D. (2003). *Statistics for Dummies*. Indianapolis, IN: Wiley Publishing.

Rush, H.M.F. (1996). "The Behavioral Sciences." In R.L. Craig, ed., *The ASTD Training and Development Handbook*. 4th edition. New York: McGraw-Hill.

Russell, J. (2003). *Leading Change Training*. Alexandria, VA: ASTD Press.

Russell, L. (2000). *Project Management for Trainers*. Alexandria, VA: ASTD Press.

————. (2005). "Leadership Development." *Infoline* No. 250508.

Russell, S. (1987). "The Management Development Process." *Infoline* No. 258711.

————. (1988). "Training and Learning Styles." *Infoline* No. 258804.

————. (1997). "Training and Learning Styles." *Infoline* No. 258804.

Russell, J., and L. Russell. (1998). *Managing Change*. Dubuque, IA: Kendall/Hunt.

————. (2005). *Strategic Planning Training*. Alexandria, VA: ASTD Press.

Russo, C.S. (1999). "Teaching SMEs to Train." *Infoline* No. 259911.

————. (2003). "Basic Training for Trainers." *Infoline* No. 258808.

————. (2005). *Early Bird Guide to ASTD Certification*. Alexandria, VA: ASTD Press.

Russo, C., and J. Mitchell, eds. (2005). "The Infoline Dictionary of Basic Trainer Terms." *Infoline* No. 250513.

Salkind, N.J. (2005). *Tests & Measurement for People Who (Think They) Hate Tests and Measurement*. Thousand Oaks, CA: Sage Publications.

Sample, J. (1993). "Legal Liability & HRD: Implications for Trainers." *Infoline* No. 259309. (Out of print.)

Sanders, E.S. (1999). "Learning Technologies." *Infoline* No. 259902.

Sanders, E.S., and S. Thiagarajan. (2001). *Performance Intervention Maps: 36 Strategies for Solving Your Organization's Problems*. Alexandria, VA: ASTD Press.

———. (2005). *Performance Intervention Maps: 39 Strategies for Solving Your Organization's Problems*. Revised edition. Alexandria, VA: ASTD Press.

Sandler, S.F., ed. (July 2005). "The Latest Business Focus for HR: Workforce Performance Management." *HRFocus*, pp. 3–4.

———. (May 2004). "Planning to Outsource." *HRFocus*, pp. 1–15.

Sasser, E.W., L.A. Schlesinger, and J.L. Heskett. (1997). *The Service Profit Chain*. New York: Free Press.

Schein, E. (1992). *Organizational Culture and Leadership*. 2nd edition. San Francisco: Jossey-Bass.

Schwarz, C.J. (1998). "Mean, Median, and Mode." Available at http://www.math.sfu.ca/~cschwarz/Stat-301/Handouts/node30.html.

Scott, B. (2000). *Consulting on the Inside*. Alexandria, VA: ASTD Press.

Scriven, M. (1967). "The Methodology of Evaluation." In R.W. Tyler, et al., eds. *Perspectives in Evaluation, American Educational Research Association Monograph Series on Curriculum Evaluation*. No. 1. Chicago: Rand McNally.

Seagraves, T. (2004). *Quick! Show Me Your Value*. Alexandria, VA: ASTD Press.

Seels, B., and R. Glasgow. (1998). *Making Instructional Design Decisions*. Upper Saddle River, NJ: Prentice-Hall.

Senge, P. (1990). *The Fifth Discipline: The Art and Practice of the Learning Organization*. New York: Doubleday/Currency.

———. (1994). *The Fifth Discipline Fieldbook*. New York: Doubleday/Currency.

———. (Fall 2000). "Lessons for Change Leaders." *Leader to Leader,* pp. 21–27

Shaffer, R. (1988). "Principles of Organization Development." *Infoline* No. 258812. (Out of print.)

Sharpe, C. (1997a). "Course Design and Development." *Infoline* No. 258905.

———. (1997b). "How to Create a Good Learning Environment." *Infoline* No. 258506

———. (1997c). "Be a Better Needs Analyst." *Infoline* No. 258502.

Shaver, W.J. (1995). "How to Build and Use a 360-Degree Feedback System." *Infoline* No. 259508.

Sheftel, P.A., and M. Bennett. (2001). "How to Resolve Conflict." *Infoline* No. 250104.

Sheinberg, M. (October, 2001). "Know Thy Learner: The Importance of Context in E-Learning Design." *Learning Circuits*. Available at http://www.learningcircuits.org.

Shiple, J. (2005). *Information Architecture Tutorial.* Available at http://webmonkey .wired.com/webmonkey/design/site_building/tutorials/tutorial1.html.

Silver, H.F., and J.R. Hanson. (1995). *Learning Styles and Strategies.* Woodbridge, NJ: The Thoughtful Education Press.

Sindell, M. (2001). "Leadership Development." *Infoline* No. 250101. (Out of print).

Six Sigma SPC's Quality Control Dictionary and Glossary. (2005). Springfield, IL: Six Sigma SPC. Available at http://www.sixsigmaspc.com/dictionary/glossary.html.

Skymark. (2005). "Affinity Diagram." Available at http://www.skymark.com/resources/tools/affinity_diagram.asp.

Smith, D., and J. Blakesell. (September 2002). "The New Strategic Six Sigma." *T+D,* pp. 45–52.

Smith, P.L., and T.J. Ragan. (2004). *Instructional Design.* 3rd edition. Hoboken, NJ: Wiley/Jossey-Bass.

Smith, W. (1989). "Managing Change: Implementation Skills." *Infoline* No. 258910. (Out of print.)

Solomon, C. (2004). "Culture Audits: Supporting Organizational Success." *Infoline* No. 250412.

Sonnenfeld, J. (1988). *The Hero's Farewell.* New York: Oxford University Press.

Sparhawk, S., and M. Schickling. (1994). "Strategic Needs Analysis." *Infoline* No. 259408.

Stevens, L. (December 2000). "Knowing What Your Company Knows." *Knowledge Management,* pp. 38–42.

Stockdale, M.S., and F.J. Crosby. (2004). *Psychology and Management of Workplace Diversity.* United Kingdom: Blackwell.

Stolovitch, H.D., and E.J. Keeps. (2002). *Telling Ain't Training.* Alexandria, VA: ASTD Press.

———. (2004). *Training Ain't Performance.* Alexandria, VA: ASTD Press.

Sugrue, B., and R.J. Rivera. (2006). *The 2005 ASTD State of the Industry Report.* Alexandria, VA: ASTD.

Sullivan, R., and J.L. Wircenski. (2001). "Effective Classroom Training Techniques." *Infoline* No. 250108.

Swanson, R. (1994). *Analysis for Improving Performance: Tools for Diagnosing Organizations and Documenting Workplace Expertise.* San Francisco: Berrett-Koehler.

Tanquist, S. (2000). "Evaluating E-Learning." *Infoline* No. 250009.

The Lectric Law Library's Lexicon on Common Law. Available at http://www.lectlaw.com/def/c070.htm.

Thiagarajan, S. (2000). "Rapid Instructional Development." In G. Piskurich, P. Beckschi, and B. Hall, eds., *The ASTD Handbook of Training Design and Delivery.* New York: McGraw-Hill.

Thomas. S.J., and P.J. Douglas. (2004). "Structured Mentoring: A Performance Approach." *Infoline* No. 250401.

Thompson, C. (1998). "Project Management: A Guide." *Infoline* No. 259004.

Titcomb, T.J. (1998). "Chaos and Complexity Theory." *Infoline* No. 259807.

Tobey, D. (2005). *Needs Assessment Basics.* Alexandria, VA: ASTD Press.

Toenniges, L., and K. Patterson. (2005). "Managing Training Projects." *Infoline* No. 250512.

Toth, T. (2003). *Technology for Trainers.* Alexandria, VA: ASTD Press.

Treacy, M., and F. Wiersema. (1995). *The Discipline of Market Leaders: Choose Your Customers, Narrow Your Focus, Dominate Your Market.* New York: Perseus Books.

Trice, H., and J. Beyer. (1993). *The Cultures of Work Organizations.* Englewood Cliffs, NJ: Prentice-Hall.

Tuckman, B., and M. Jensen. (1977). "Stages of Small Group Development Revisited." *Group and Organizational Studies,* pp. 419–427.

Tufte, E.R. (2001). *Visual Display of Quantitative Information.* Cheshire, CN: Graphics Press.

Tunick, R.H. (2002). "Career Counseling: Traditional Approaches." West Virginia University white paper. Available at http://www.hre.wvu.edu/rtunick02/Career%20Counseling.htm.

Tyler, R. (1949). *Basic Principles of Curriculum and Instruction.* Chicago: University of Chicago Press.

U.S. Census Bureau. (2001). "200 Years of U.S. Census Taking: Population and Housing Questions 1790–1990." Washington, D.C.: Bureau of the Census, Department of Commerce.

U.S. Copyright Office. (2006). "About Copyright." Available at http://www.copyright.gov/circs/circ1.html.

Van Tiem, D., and J. Rosenzweig. (2005). "Performance Excellence Through Partnering." *Infoline* No. 250504.

———. (2006). "Appreciative Inquiry." *Infoline* No. 250601.

Verardo, D. (1997). "Managing the Strategic Planning Process." *Infoline* No. 259710.

Vodvarka, J.A. "Information Architecture: Designing the User Experience." Available at http://web.archive.org/web/20010604212326/http://www.luminant.com/IMAGES/WP_InformationArchitecture.pdf.

Voosen, D., and P. Conneely. (2002). "Building Learning Communities." *Infoline* No. 250208.

Vrooman, R. (1997). "Group Process Tools." *Infoline* No. 259407.

Waagen, A.K. (1997). "Essentials for Evaluation." *Infoline* No. 259705.

———. (1998). "Task Analysis." *Infoline* No. 259808.

———. (2000). "How to Budget Training." *Infoline* No. 250007.

Wagner, S. (August 2000). "Retention: Finders Keepers." *Training & Development,* p. 64.

Waterman, R.H., Jr. (1987). *The Renewal Factor: How to Get and Keep the Competitive Edge.* New York: Bantam.

Watts, A.G., et al (1996). *Rethinking Careers in Education and Guidance.* United Kingdom: Routledge.

Webopedia: Online Computer Dictionary for Computer and Internet Terms and Definitions. (2006). Jupitermedia Corporation. Available at http://www.webopedia.com.

Weisbord, M. (1987). *Productive Workplaces.* San Francisco: Jossey-Bass.

Wheatley, M. (1994). *Leadership and the New Science.* San Francisco, CA: Berrett-Koehler.

Wheatley, M., and M. Kellner-Rogers. (1996). *A Simpler Way.* San Francisco, CA: Berrett-Koehler.

Whitbourne, S., and C. Weinstock. (1979). *Adult Development.* New York: Holt, Rinehart & Winston.

Wholey, J.S., H.P. Hatry, and K.E. Newcomer. (2004). *Handbook of Practical Program Evaluation.* 2nd edition. San Francisco: Jossey-Bass.

Wiggenhorn, W.A. (1996). "Organization and Management of Training." In R.L. Craig, ed., *The ASTD Training and Development Handbook.* 4th edition. New York: McGraw-Hill.

Wiig, K.M. (1997). "Knowledge Management: Where Did It Come from, and Where Will It Go?" *Journal of Expert Systems with Applications,* pp. 1-14.

———. (2004). *People-Focused Knowledge Management: How Effective Decision Making Leads to Corporate Success.* Jordan Hill, Oxford: Elservier Butterworth-Heinemann.

Wikipedia, the Free Encyclopedia. (2006). Wikimedia Foundation, Inc. Available at http://en.Wikipedia.org/wiki/Main_Page.

Willmore, J. (2004). *Performance Basics.* Alexandria, VA: ASTD Press.

Wilmoth, F.S., C. Prigmore, and M. Bray. (September 2002). "HPT Models: An Overview of the Major Models in the Field." *Performance Improvement,* pp. 14–22.

Wircenski, J.L., and R.L. Sullivan. (1998). "Make Every Presentation a Winner." *Infoline* No. 258606.

Withers, B. (2000). "Basic Training: Getting Ready to Present." In G. Piskurich, P. Beckschi, and B. Hall, eds. *The ASTD Handbook of Training Design and Delivery.* New York: McGraw-Hill.

Younger, S.M. (1999). "How to Develop a Vision." *Infoline* No. 259107.

Zaleznik, A. (January 2004). "Managers and Leaders: Are They Different?" *Harvard Business Review,* pp. 74–81.

Zemke, R. (2000). *Generations at Work.* New York: AMACOM.

Zulauf, C.A. (1997). "Systems Thinking." *Infoline* No. 259703.

ASTD Learning System Editorial Staff

Director: Cat Russo
Manager: Mark Morrow
Editors: Tora Estep, Jennifer Mitchell

Contributing Editors
April Davis, Stephanie Sussan

Proofreading
April Davis, Eva Kaplan-Leiserson

Graphic Design
Kathleen Schaner

ASTD (American Society for Training & Development) is the world's largest association dedicated to workplace learning and performance professionals. ASTD's 70,000 members and associates come from more than 100 countries and thousands of organizations--multinational corporations, medium-sized and small businesses, government, academia, consulting firms, and product and service suppliers.

ASTD marks its beginning in 1944 when the organization held its first annual conference. In recent years, ASTD has widened the industry's focus to connect learning and performance to measurable results, and is a sought-after voice on critical public policy issues.

Linking People,
Learning & Performance

Thomson NETg Staff

Solutions Manager: Robyn Rickenbach
Director: John Pydyn

Contributing Writers
Lynn Lewis, Dawn Rader:

Contributing Editors
Lisa Lord, Kim Lindros, Karen Day

Thomson NETg is a global enterprise-learning leader offering an integrated suite of learning modalities and content, next generation technologies, and supportive strategic services designed to align with key organizational initiatives. NETg clients ensure continual, enterprise-wide acquisition of knowledge and information while lowering the overall cost of learning for the organization. With the KnowledgeNow Suite, clients are able to develop, customize, host, deliver, and report on engaging learning initiatives, delivered in blended modalities. Thousands of leading companies and government agencies around the world rely on Thomson NETg to achieve important business productivity and performance improvements. From healthcare to telecommunications, manufacturing to pharmaceuticals, retail to financial services, military operations to human services, NETg KnowledgeNow consistently delivers.

NETg is backed by The Thomson Corporation, a global enterprise comprised of a vast array of world-renowned publishing and information assets in the areas of academics, business and government, financial services, science and health care, and the law.